The Moon and More

Dear Grover & Frances (Fannie),

Thank you for being like a mom and dad to Virginia, and I think it's incredible that you made the long trip to Longview to be at our wedding.

I thought you might enjoy parts of this book — Grover, the space sections and maybe the sports sections, and Fannie, the poetry and song lyrics, etc.

Your wonderful, positive attitudes and personalities are an inspiration to me. May God continue to bless and keep you and yours.

Love,
David

You're on page 124.

The Moon and More

✦

The Story of David Alexander and His Family and Friends

James David Alexander Family

iUniverse, Inc.

New York Lincoln Shanghai

The Moon and More
The Story of David Alexander and His Family and Friends

iUniverse books may be ordered through booksellers or by contacting:

iUniverse
2021 Pine Lake Road, Suite 100
Lincoln, NE 68512
www.iuniverse.com
1-800-Authors (1-800-288-4677)

ISBN: 978-0-595-44555-4 (pbk)
ISBN: 978-0-595-88882-5 (ebk)

Printed in the United States of America

This book is dedicated to all those who have positively affected David's life, including family, friends, ministers, coaches, teachers, and others, plus those who have helped keep our nation free, safe, and successful, especially those who have given their lives for these causes.

A Special Thanks to Virginia for her patience and understanding while David spent many hours completing this book and for her help in editing and proofing the book although most of the book's information involves people and events prior to her knowing David.

Contents

Howard & Mary Ann Jones & Gin
Troy & Michelle LeBlanc
Don & Elaine Pinkerton(s)
Maxie & Mae Richards(s)
Roy & Ann Smalley(s)
Neal & Mary Alice Watkins(s)
Ken & Tricia Young

Dallas & Nelda Anderson
Rick & Karen Anderson
James & Mim Blackwood(s)
Hal & Pat Boone
Les & Merideth Chambers
Bob & Linda/Gay Doan
Bill & Anita Durham
Grover & Frances Gaskin
Tommy & Sherry Herndon
Pat and Joann Hoffmaster
Jim Irwin
Mark & Anna Johnson(s)
Bob & Pat Kehl
Jerry & Kathy Lanan
George & Carlee Marcom
Neil & Pat Marshall
David/Wayne & Sue (Leake) Mitchell(s)
Earl Wayne & Carol Miller(s)
Virtie Miller
Don & Millie McLeod
Winnie Newman
Ware & Bonnie Phillips(s)
Ross & Jennifer Rainwater
Ron & Donna Sanford(s)
Cody Terry & Family
Caroline Walker and Family
Ed & Glenna Wandling

Shirley Epperson

Karen Duran

Kay Penick

Martha "Mot" Parten

Gail Rambo

Diana Duke

Cherry Hanicak

Nancy Nail

Zelda Morris

Grace McMullin Blanton

Joed Stites Brady

Royce Toler Butler

Pat Greer Davis

Jimmye Looper Ferrell

Shirley Davis Goss

Shirley Rogers King

Nona Roark Stansell

Judy Thompson Shavers

Shirley Smith Manning

Judy Allison Stuart

Sue Huntley Yoder

Pat Young Daniels

Pete Ferris

Fred Roberson

Jimmy Wilkins

Bob & Derrith Bondurant

Carl & Winnie Breckel

Cindy Freeman

Jack & Debbie Goetz

Laney & Emily Johnson

Foreword

David was born with an abnormal heart and unfortunate blood chemistry and miraculously survived pneumonia as an infant, and yet became an outstanding athlete as a young man, later helped figure out how to put men on the Moon and design and fly the Space Shuttle during his NASA career, and became an amateur poet, songwriter, and Gospel quartet singer. He was blessed with two beautiful wives, a wonderful family, and many great friends.

This is his story and includes facts, memories, beliefs, and opinions that hopefully will have historical and other meaning to current and especially future generations of his family and friends. He has often wished he had more information about his ancestors and other deceased friends, but such information existed mainly by word-of-mouth and is no longer available. A major objective of this book is to put in one place such information about himself and, to a lesser extent, about his family and friends.

Another major objective of this book is to document how God has blessed a regular guy who has tried to serve and obey Him, and not to boast or impress. Although the book is basically an autobiography, most of it is written in the third person instead of the first person to enhance the accomplishment of this objective.

David has been in his mid-60's during the completion of this book, and he is the source of much of its information, either directly or indirectly, although most of his sports career information and much of the other factual information were taken from other documentation.

The information is organized such that the various subjects and people addressed can be readily accessed by using either the Contents sections and subsections (which are also used within the body of the book) or page numbers.

Photos are included near the end of the book in Section 6.

Summary of David's Life

James David Alexander was born November 22, 1939, in Longview, Texas, to George Wiseman and Olga Mildred (Howeth) Alexander. He grew up in the country on an oil field lease where his dad was a field superintendent for an oil company. David miraculously survived pneumonia as an infant and was a somewhat shy but happy young lad.

He attended White Oak Schools from 1st through 12th grade. He was a good student from the start and decided at an early age to try to become the best student and athlete that he could be. He was selected as the top all-round student of his senior class and was also the class salutatorian and the student body president. He starred on state championship teams in each football, basketball, and track and is among the most decorated high school athletes in White Oak High School's history. Nearly fifty years later (at the time of this writing) he still holds school sports records in the four sports in which he participated—football, basketball, track, and baseball. He was recruited for football, basketball, and/or track by about 20 major universities and chose to attend Baylor on a football and track scholarship. Because of (at that time) undiagnosed stamina problems, he gave up football during his sophomore year, but he ran on some of the fastest collegian relay teams in the nation during his varsity track career. He was part of two outdoor track and field conference championship teams, two of only three thus far in Baylor's history. He was also a Baylor honor student and earned a Bachelor of Science Degree in math/physics in 1962.

After working for seven months in missile research at the Department of Defense Naval Ordnance Lab in Corona, California, he began a 32-year career with NASA at the (now) Johnson Space Center in Houston in February 1963. He was vitally involved in figuring out how to put men on the moon and later in designing the Space Shuttle and its flights. He became a specialist in how to maneuver a spacecraft, and more specifically, in how to bring two spacecraft together (rendezvous) in space. He was also involved in several other NASA programs, including the early planning for the International Space Station during the last few years of his career.

On February 16, 1963, two weeks after beginning his employment with NASA, David married the beautiful Sandra (Sandy) Bingham, the younger daughter of H. E. (Bill) and Aline Bingham, a prominent White Oak family. Sandy was one year behind David and was also a graduate of both White Oak and Baylor (B.A. Elementary Education, 1963). Although they knew of each other from childhood, David and Sandy actually did not start dating until later college years. Sandy was a teacher for 27 years in the Houston/NASA area.

David and Sandy's wonderful marriage ended on October 18, 2000, when Sandy lost her 3½-year battle with recurrent breast cancer.

David and Sandy parented two wonderful, successful children. Millicent (Milli) Lauree' was born August 30, 1968, and David Gregory (Greg) was born December 10, 1970. Milli was selected the Outstanding All Round Student when she graduated in 1986 from Clear Creek High School (one of the largest high schools in Texas at the time). Four years later she was selected as an Outstanding Senior Woman as a Baylor University graduate. In 1993 she received a law degree from Baylor Law School. She is now a full-time mother and the wife of David Lee Jacks in Fort Worth. Their first child, David Lee Jacks II, David A.'s only grandson, was born October 17, 2000, a few hours before Sandy passed away. Their second child, Laura Alexis, was born on September 29, 2002.

Greg was honored as Student of the Year and as an Outstanding High School Student of America during his school years. From his early teens, he was a computer whiz. He is now one of the most highly respected and successful computer specialists in the NASA arena. He and his wife, Catherine (Cathy), are the parents of three of David's precious granddaughters, Ali, Caitlin, and Megan. Ali died in an auto accident in April 1997 at age 2, but is still very much in everyone's hearts and thoughts. Caitlin was born on June 19, 1998, and Megan was born on April 7, 2000.

When Milli was age 6 and Greg was age 4, it was discovered that Milli could sing harmony and Greg could sing melody, and the David Alexanders began singing as a family group. Sandy and Greg sang melody, Milli sang harmony above the melody, and David sang harmony below the melody. They weren't Carnegie Hall quality but were quite a novelty and sang in church services and at banquets around the Houston area for 5-6 years. Then the kids became "too grown up" to sing with mom and dad, but it was special while it lasted. Although neither David nor Sandy had quality singing voices, both Milli and Greg became outstanding vocalists. David says that he asked the Lord for a solo voice, and the Lord gave him two.

David became a Christian at age 7 and became an ordained Baptist deacon at age 36. His other main interest in addition to family, friends, space, and sports has been Christian music, especially Gospel male quartet music. He has composed 14 original songs (most for male quartets) and, beginning at age 12, has sung in several quartets. He managed and sang baritone with The Master's Vessels Gospel quartet for 12½ years while in the Houston/NASA area, and Sandy was their pianist. They averaged about 40 engagements per year as a part-time group and published seven projects (tapes). David currently sings baritone with Four-Ever His (formerly named Thee Mobb Quad) of Longview's Mobberly Baptist Church, and Sandy also played for them until shortly before her death. David will quickly tell you that he is not a soloist and barely has the quality to be a "baritone blender," but he does possess a natural ear for all harmony and the gift of organization and leadership and the talent to arrange and compose music for voices. He has also written quite a few poems through the years, most of them for loved ones and friends or for special events.

During the first 27 years of David's space career, he worked directly for NASA as a civil servant, but during the last five years, after taking an early retirement from NASA, he worked for a NASA contractor, Barrios Technology. During about half of his total space career, he was a technical manager at various levels, but during the exciting years of Gemini and Apollo, he was directly involved in the incredible technical developments and achievements as a front-line mission designer. Although he received a large number of awards and honors during his career for both technical and managerial contributions, his most cherished award is probably one that he received in 1993 about 1½ years before his retirement. He was the annual recipient of the Barrios' Emy Award, signifying outstanding citizenship within the NASA Johnson Space Center community.

At age 37 David underwent his first coronary bypass surgery. He had been told a few years earlier that he had an unfortunate lipid chemistry that normally led to advanced heart disease and often death in the mid-to-late 40's. At the time of his first surgery he was told that part of his coronary artery structure was also abnormally small. His doctors were amazed that he had been a good athlete because of the lack of stamina that this heart abnormality should have caused. In fact, they said that it was probably a miracle that he had not dropped dead of a heart attack while competing in high school and college. At last David had an explanation for the stamina problems he experienced beginning in his late teens while participating in sports.

David retired from the space program in January 1995 at age 55, about seven months after undergoing coronary bypass surgery for the second time. Severe complications were involved, requiring a total of 46 days in the hospital, and the doctors highly recommended retirement. Sandy retired at the end of the semester in December 1994, and they moved back to their original hometown (Longview) area.

Amid David's happy and highly blessed life, there have been some very tough and sad times. In addition to his own health problems, Sandy was initially diagnosed with breast cancer in 1986. Though the chemotherapy treatments temporarily diminished her outward beauty, it greatly strengthened her faith and inward beauty. For almost ten years she was symptom-free, but the cancer reoccurred in early 1997 (about two years after their retirements), and she valiantly fought the disease for 3½ years until her death.

Soon after Sandy's cancer recurrence, their first grandchild, Ali, died in an auto accident while she and Greg and Cathy were returning home to League City from a visit in Longview. The accident occurred when their car began hydroplaning during a horrendous rainstorm. Cathy's injuries were very serious, but she completely recovered. Other than Sandy's death, this is surely the most terrible thing that has ever happened to the David Alexanders.

In spite of these major downers, David and Sandy's retirement was good overall. They traveled often after retirement, including four cruises (they took about a dozen other cruises prior to retirement), a coach tour in Western Europe, and several auto trips within the States with best friends and relatives. They were members of a great church, Mobberly Baptist, and participated in its tremendous music ministry as health permitted. David is still an active member there and serves as a member of three singing groups: the 150-voice PraiSingers, the 24-voice men's ensemble called the Men of Praise, and the Four-Ever His Gospel male quartet.

David also still speaks periodically on a voluntary basis about his experiences with NASA to various groups, including students, service clubs, chambers of commerce, etc.

Several months after Sandy's death, David became acquainted (through Mobberly Baptist) with a lovely lady, Virginia Ouzts, whose first spouse had also died from cancer in mid-2000. During the following year or so, David and Virginia became good friends and then close companions. They realized in the summer of 2002 that they truly loved each other and should become husband and wife. They were married on January 11, 2003, at Mobberly Baptist. Over 200 friends and relatives attended, about twice as many as expected, causing the Lord to apparently send a miracle relative to stretching the reception food to the limit. Much more is included about Virginia and her family in Section 2.2.

In late 2005, David received one of the greatest honors of his life. He was inducted into the Baylor Letterwinners' Wall of Honor "because of extraordinary recognition and honor brought to Baylor by his career and other life accomplish-ments." Among the 300 or so in attendance at the combination Wall of Honor and Hall of Fame induction banquet were Virginia, Milli and Greg and their spouses, Virginia's daughter, Julie, and her husband and son, and several of David's teammates and other special Baylor friends. David was the only 2005 inductee to the Wall of Honor and only the eighth to be inducted since its incep-tion in 2001. Other previous inductees include Hayden Fry, renowned college football coach, and Clyde Hart, great Baylor and Olympic track coach. The next day David and the five 2005 Hall of Fame inductees were introduced on national TV just prior to the Texas-Baylor football game. The following fall, they were honorees at Baylor Homecoming and were featured in the Homecoming parade.

1

Details of David's Life, Beliefs, Etc.

1.1 EARLY YEARS

1.1.1 Many Miracles Granted

David was born in the old Markham Hospital in Longview on November 22, 1939, a year or so after his parents, George and Olga, moved to an oil field lease in White Oak. When he was three months old, he had severe pneumonia, and his doctor said only a miracle could save him. So the first miracle in David's life occurred then. Fifty-four years later, after his second coronary bypass surgery, the doctors told his family that the chances of his surviving were very slim, and another miracle was sent down. There is no telling how many miracles were granted between these two miracles. The doctors later told David that because of his abnormal heart, with which he was born, that it was a miracle that he didn't drop dead of a heart attack every time he seriously competed in sports.

Soon after David began to walk, he wandered out behind the car as his dad began to back out of the garage. His mom screamed from the kitchen, but his dad didn't hear her. Their collie dog, cleverly named Collie, grabbed David by the sleeve and pulled him from behind the backing car. A year or so later, David disappeared and his parents found him out in the pasture. A big bull was 20 feet from him with Collie in between them barking like crazy. So there are a couple of other miracles sent through a pet dog. A few years later when David was a Cub Scout, he entered Collie in a contest as "Best Cared-For Dog." As far as David was concerned, he cared for Collie as much as anyone could care for a dog. Of course, the "Best Cared-For" category meant "the best groomed," and Collie probably hadn't had a bath, other than in the creek, for months. The judges, with big grins on their faces, suggested that David switch Collie to the "Friendliest

Dog" category. He did, and Collie won. When Collie died several years later, David wrote a theme about him for his freshman English class. Nearly everyone in the class was shedding tears by the time he finished reading it.

1.1.2 Early Memories

Although David was not quite 2 years old when Pearl Harbor happened, he remembers it. He also remembers how pretty he thought his mom was when he was only 3-4 years old. He would sit in church when only 5-6 years old and quietly play football or basketball using two small strips of paper as the players and a songbook as the playing field or court. At 8-9 years old, he would listen to ball games on the radio and imagine becoming a good athlete someday. As a lad he often hiked through the woods or climbed the oil derricks surrounding his home while thinking about success and making a significant contribution to mankind.

David's parents were not overly affectionate outwardly, but he never doubted their love for him or for each other. They almost never got upset with each other or about much of anything else. David did get a few whippings (switchings) from George when he really deserved them, but he never thought George was being mean or hateful. David developed a great respect for his parents early on, and one of his main goals was to always please them. They greatly encouraged him in all aspects of his life—Christian example, grades, sports, music, etc.

1.1.3 Fun Family Times

George often took David quail hunting with him starting when David was about five. When Maggie, their bird dog, would find a covey of quail and they would fly, David would hit the deck. George, who was an excellent marksman, would usually get 2 or 3 of them. David was never as good a marksman as George, probably to some extent because David never had much time to hunt due to his participation in the athletic sports.

George started playing catch with David when David was 3-4 years old and knocking flyballs to him and shooting baskets with him when David was 7-8 years old. David says he never remembers George being too busy to play catch or knock flyballs or shoot baskets.

Among his favorite times as a young lad were the family trips to Oklahoma to see his Alexander grandparents and other Alex relatives. A hug from Cousin Anita was worth the 6-hour trip, and playing ball in Grandma and Grandpa's yard with all the cousins was much fun. David also enjoyed going to visit Big Mama, Olga's mother, and other Howeth relatives east of Henderson, Texas.

Some of the special Longview-area family friends during those early years are mentioned alphabetically below. All of the parents were in David's parents' generation and are now deceased, but some of the children are still friends with whom David communicates periodically.

The Fletcher Austins—Visited in each other's homes often after church at Spring Hill Baptist; had two sons and five daughters; son, Johnny, was a year younger than David.

The N. L. Barretts—After-church friends at Emmanuel Baptist (White Oak); grandparents of 1969 Miss Texas, Dana Dowell, via daughter Barbarah.

The Eldon Clarks—Son, Gene, and David were good buddies as pre-teenagers at Spring Hill Baptist, and Gene is now a leading citizen in the Spring Hill community.

The Tom Dicksons—Neighbors across the field and song leader at Spring Hill Baptist; son, Gene, was the bass in the first quartet David sang in at age 12.

The L. C. Fishers—Parents of David's first "girlfriend," Dixie; had two sons who were 16-17 years older than Dixie. David's pet name for Mrs. Fisher was Jitter (other) Momma.

The Archie Halls—Friends at Emmanuel Baptist; daughter, Nancy, was one of David's special friends during pre-teenage years.

"Uncle" Earl & "Aunt" Amy Meadows—Friends at Spring Hill Baptist; babysat David some; Earl was a Gospel quartet enthusiast.

The Perrys—Neighbors up the road; had two sons, Jerry and Douglas (Bubba), who were 2-3 years younger than David, and they played together a lot during pre-teenage years.

The Charlie Smiths—Nearest neighbor (about 150 yards through the woods); she child-sat David some when he was 4-6 years old; he called her "Mud" (short for mother).

The Gene Tevebaughs—Gene came to East Texas at the same time as David's dad and worked for the same oil company for many years; had four sons who were all good high school football players at East Mountain.

The Don Treadwells—Friends at Spring Hill Baptist; son, J. D., and David were good friends in early years; J. D. became very good high school basketball player.

The Dewey Warnicks—Gave David his first lawn-mowing job when he was about age 10; Dewey stayed at the hospital and prayed continuously when David

almost died with pneumonia at age 3 months—probably believed in divine healing, thank God!

1.2 ATHLETIC CAREER

Most of the information about stats, honors, records, etc., in the sections below
came from other documents about White Oak sports (particularly Joe Lee
Smith's "Beneath the Towering Oil Wells") and about Baylor sports. David is
quick to say that he probably received far more honors during his time at White
Oak than he deserved, and that some of the honors he received were probably
deserved as much or more by some of his teammates.

1.2.1 Childhood Years

David's dad, George, started giving David sports items when David was three
years old. By the time David was about eight, he had a football, a basketball and
goal, baseballs and bats, and equipment to go with each of these sports. George
and David started playing catch when David was about three, and by the time
David was an early teenager, George was knocking him fly balls of 300 feet.

There was no organized little kid sports in the Longview area until Little
League Baseball started in 1951, when David was 11. Prior to then, there were
occasional sports activities at church. A teacher-coach, Mr. Hunt, at Spring Hill
would supply a few bats and balls for a few games during the summers when
David was 9-10, and David, who was tall for his age, was usually one of the
younger kids involved and typically played with guys 2-3 years older. That was to
become a trend in his life for years to come.

1.2.2 Little League and Other Summer Baseball

As stated above, Little League Baseball started in the Longview area when David
was 11. In those years sadly not every kid made the teams, and that first year there
was only one league in the entire Longview area. White Oak was one of four rural
teams, and Longview proper had four teams. There was only one ballpark, which
was off Mobberly Avenue in Longview.

In the first game of the year, David hit a home run off the best pitcher in the
league, who later pitched several no-hitters. David thereby holds the distinction
of hitting the first home run in the history of Longview-area Little League Base-

ball. However, although he was one of the good hitters in the league, David was not selected for the All Star team that first year, as mostly 12 year olds were selected. Except for his freshman year in high school (when he played on the varsity as a freshman in four sports), that first Little League team turned out to be the only summer league team or high school team on which he played that he was not selected an All Star, All District, or higher.

The next year, David's 12-year-old year, a separate league was started for the rural communities, and Longview had their own league. The White Oak Giants went undefeated, and David amassed the league's top batting average (625). He and five of his teammates made the All Star team. They defeated the Longview All Stars but lost in the second round of the playoffs.

David later played on White Oak's Pony League (13 and 14 year olds) and American Legion (15 and 16 year olds) teams, advancing to the state tournament in Houston as a 14-year-old Pony League All Star. He began pitching as a 16 year old both in summer league and in high school. Although he was a winning pitcher, he was never the ace of the pitching staff, and he made the All Star and All District teams as a centerfielder. He typically led each team on which he played in batting average.

1.2.3 Junior High Sports

David started playing football in public school in the 6th grade and began playing basketball and running track in the 7th grade, which were the first years these sports were offered in public school or elsewhere back then. Baseball was not offered in public school until high school varsity.

Probably because he was one of the biggest guys on the team, David played tackle on the 6th grade football team, and they played only 3-4 games against other schools. He had a helmet without a chinstrap, and nearly every time he made a tackle, his helmet would fly off. Such would be grounds for a lawsuit in today's world. He once blocked a punt and picked up his helmet, which had come off, on his way to recover the football for a touchdown.

David started on the freshmen football team (end) and basketball team (center-forward) as a 7th grader. In his first basketball game, he was the game's leading scorer and made two free throws in the last few seconds to win the game by one point. Possibly only a few folks, including his junior high basketball coach, Moon Mullins (who taught David his free throw form), might have guessed then that David would eventually become White Oak High School's all-time leader in career points and free throw percentage. Later that 7th-grade year, in his first ever freshmen basketball tournament, David was selected to the All Tournament Team, the first of nine All Tournament Teams during his junior high and high school years.

That 7th-grade spring, it was discovered that David was the fastest sprinter on the freshmen track team. He pulled a muscle long-jumping at the freshmen district meet, his first ever official track meet, and was not able to participate in the 100 and relays, but this was to be one of only 2 or 3 track meets throughout his 10-year track career (including college) in which he would not win or place high in one or more individual or relay events.

During his 8th-grade year, David starred on district championship freshmen teams in each football, basketball, and track. He made All Tournament in the three invitational basketball tournaments in which White Oak played and won by defeating highly-favored teams from larger schools. An especially memorable time occurred at the Carlisle tournament (where White Oak's coach, Moon Mullins, had graduated from high school). After the semi-final games, won by Kilgore (Class 4A) and White Oak (Class A), the Kilgore coach told Coach Mullins that his Kilgore team shouldn't have entered the tournament because the rest of the teams weren't near Kilgore's level. They had won all their games in the tournament by 30 or more points. Coach Mullins replied, "Well, I'm sure that you're right, but since we're already here, we might as well play the finals." In the championship game, White Oak beat Kilgore by 15 points. Four of the starters on that team were also starters on the team that won the Class A high school state championship four years later. White Oak later won the Longview freshmen tournament by soundly defeating a couple of 4A schools, including Denton, who had been highly-favored to win that tournament. The Longview tournament directors were so upset that they put three Denton players on the All Tournament team and put only two White Oak players on the team, David and Mike Cobb.

In the district track meet that spring, David won the 100 and anchored the winning sprint and mile relays, a feat he would repeat many times in years to come.

1.2.4 High School Freshman and Sophomore Years

In the early summer of 1954, White Oak High School's varsity coaches (Cotton Miles, football and baseball, Moon Mullins, football and track, and Emil Hanicak, basketball) paid a visit to David and his parents. They said that they were convinced that both David and White Oak sports would be better off in the long run if David would play these four varsity sports as a freshman instead of playing on the freshmen teams. The experience he would gain would be extremely valuable for future years even if he did not become a varsity starter as a freshman. At age 14 David was already 6'2" and 165 lbs, and was one of the fastest athletes at White Oak. The decision came down to whether he was willing to forgo being a star player on the freshmen teams. He probably would have become a quarterback had he competed on the freshmen football team, and that likely would have changed the direction of his sports career. Fortunately, it was decided that he would move on up to the varsity in all four sports—football, basketball, baseball, and track. Although he played nearly half of the time, he did not become a starter in football that freshman year, but he did become a starter in the other three sports. His four varsity letters he earned as a freshman resulted in his becoming the only White Oak male athlete ever to earn 16 varsity letters. The experience gained that freshman year contributed greatly to his later receiving many honors and in his setting a large number of White Oak sports records, several which still stand after almost 50 years (see Section 1.2.16.1).

White Oak's football team that fall lost only one game (non-district) but was forced to forfeit four district games because of an ineligible player (who played very little) based on a strange UIL rule which no longer applies. White Oak beat Gaston, the team that represented the district, by 21 points.

In basketball, David did not start the first 5-6 games of his freshman year. About the seventh game, the starting center got into foul trouble early and David got to play most of the game. He scored about 25 points, got a bunch of rebounds, and White Oak won big. David started the next game and then every game for the remainder of his high school career. That freshman year, White Oak was runner-up to Troup in district, and Troup went on to win the Class A state championship. In those years, only the district champion advanced to the play-offs in each sport. The second-best team in a district could have been the second-best team in the state and never get to the playoffs.

In baseball as a freshman, David started every game in centerfield for the regional championship team. Regional was as far as Class A teams could advance in baseball in those years.

In track, David did not run the 100 as a freshman but won the 220 in the district meet and a couple of other meets. He won fourth in the district high jump, the only time he ever entered the high jump. He ran the second leg on the sprint relay and started the mile relay. Both relay teams won most of their races throughout the year and made it to the state meet, placing third in the sprint relay and fifth in the mile relay.

So the foundation was set for one of White Oak's all-time best all-round individual high school careers. But David was just one of 6-7 exceptional all-round White Oak athletes in the late-1950's that led in the accomplishment of what is often referred to as The Super Sports Era of the Late-1950's (see Section 1.2.10).

During David's sophomore year, he made first-team All District in football, basketball, and baseball, and was district and regional champ in the 100 and sprint relay (which he anchored). White Oak's football team had only 5-6 seniors, and injuries pulled them down to a 5-5 record, one of the worst in White Oak's history to that time. In spite of their team record, David led the district in receiving and receiving TD's. He scored on long TD passes on the first or second play of the game in 4-5 games and totaled about 500 receiving yards for the season.

David was the leading scorer on a good 1956 basketball team, which again was district runner-up to Troup, who again advanced far into the playoffs. In a pre-district game against Spring Hill, David scored about 35 points while running a fever of about 102. He finished the season with about 500 points, which helped propel him toward being White Oak's all-time leader in career points.

In baseball, David reportedly compiled the highest batting average (565) in East Texas that spring (and in White Oak's history) and was one of the few sophomores ever chosen to the first-team All East Texas Team (centerfielder). In those years, the All East Texas team combined all classifications (B through 4A) and encompassed both the greater Longview and Tyler areas. White Oak again went as far as possible by winning the regional championship.

1.2.5 High School Junior Year

Because of his varsity experience as a freshman, David's junior year was equivalent to a senior year relative to experience and confidence. The year began with White Oak's football team ranked high in Class A. By mid-season, they rose to Number 1 in the state rankings and remained there to the end of the regular season by going undefeated and leading the state in scoring. David compiled about 800 receiving yards (probably still a single-season school record) and scored about 20 touchdowns (5 in one game). However, Linden pulled off a major upset in the bi-district game, defeating White Oak 26-13. Two of White Oak's key players were out with injuries, but Linden simply outplayed the Roughnecks, especially in the second half. David, as an end-receiver, and senior tackle Mike Cobb both were selected first-team All State, and both made first-team All District and All East Texas, along with a couple of their other teammates.

The early exit from the football playoffs proved to be a plus for the 1957 basketball season. White Oak won the Class A state championship while compiling a 31-4 record. Two of their loses were to district foe Quitman, probably the second best Class A team in the state. One of the loses to Quitman was in the Longview Invitational Tournament, subsequently won by Quitman. White Oak won all of their state playoff games by 10 points or more. Prior to district play, they defeated several 4A and 3A teams (Longview, Kilgore, Nacogdoches, etc.) by 15-20 points. Most of these higher-classification teams were played in invitational tournaments in which David made All Tournament. The Roughnecks may have been among the best 3-4 teams in the state, including all classifications. David led the team in scoring with 629 points. He and senior Mike Cobb (leading rebounder) were selected first-team State Tournament All Tournament Team. Unbelievably, neither made first-team Associated Press (AP) All State. Cobb made second-team and David received honorable mention. White Oak's coach, Emil Hanicak, was terribly upset and sent a letter to the AP expressing his disbelief that a team could win the state championship, winning all it's play-off games by 10-15 points, and then not land a single player on the first-team All State Team. This protest letter apparently did some good for the future, as five Roughnecks made first-team All State during the next 7-8 years, including David in 1958, and several others made second-team All State during this period.

David and 7-8 of the other all-round Roughneck athletes participated in both baseball and track in the spring. That required somewhat of a time-juggling process, but was doable. The only year White Oak did not win district in baseball during David's four years was his junior year. That year they lost district by one game by one run to Judson, who produced three major college baseball players from its team. David batted over 300 and made All District.

White Oak won both district and regional in track, and David won the 100 and anchored both relays (440 and mile) at each meet. At the state meet, Cobb spiked the heel of David's shoe during the final hand-off of the 440 relay, pulling the heel of the shoe off. David kicked the shoe off and ran most of the anchor leg with only one shoe on, and they still barely failed to qualify for the finals.

The Roughnecks did qualify for the mile relay finals with about the third best time. That night at the motel David awoke with a bad hurting in his chest and felt so bad that he slept only a few hours. The next day he lay under the stands at Memorial Stadium until time for the mile relay, the last event of the state meet. When Coach Mullins asked if David thought he could run, David decided to try to warm up. He could not run anywhere near full speed and his chest hurt severely. It was almost time for the race, and it looked hopeless. David looked to

Heaven and asked the Lord to help him run and do his best—and if so, he would tell of the experience for the rest of his life. David began to feel strongly impressed that he should try to run the race, although he still felt bad and his chest was hurting. As Cobb, who ran the third leg, took the baton a yard in first place, David shed his warm-ups and stepped onto the track. Suddenly the hurting stopped and he felt ready to run. David took the baton from Cobb with about a one yard lead. At about the 220 mark, the Stinett anchorman began to pass David and got about a half stride ahead. David's dad, George, was at home listening on the radio. He later told David that the announcer said, "There goes Stinett passing White Oak—no, wait, White Oak is holding Stinett off, not letting Stinett cut in." George said he almost had a heart attack. Well, David did hold off the Stinett runner all the way around the final curve, and then found enough to pull about a half-stride ahead and managed to hold that lead to the finish line. Because of the excitement, David felt okay on the winners stand and during the team meal afterward, and then he slept most of the 6-hour trip home to White Oak. However, the next morning his temperature was 102. The doctor diagnosed double-pneumonia, and David missed about a week of school. But several times in later years, he told of this "miracle," and he hopes that it's inclusion in this book will preserve the story for many years to come.

1.2.6 High School Senior Year

David became one of the most recognized and decorated high school athletes in Texas (particularly East Texas) during his senior year. He starred on state championship teams in football and track and also on district championship teams in basketball and baseball. He was selected first-team All State in both football and basketball, making him the only Roughneck ever to be so honored, as well as reportedly the only athlete from any of the seven Gregg County high schools ever to be so honored. In fact, only a few athletes in the history of Texas high school sports have ever made first-team All State in both football and basketball. David's All State football selection was by a unanimous vote, and made him the only Roughneck ever selected first-team All State in football two different years, even though former pro football players Max McGee, Russell Wayt, Mike Barber, Sam and Byron Hunt, and three others from earlier years were all White Oak products.

David again made All District in football, basketball, and baseball, making him the only Roughneck ever to be selected All District three years in all three of these sports. He was selected All East Texas in football for the second year. He was probably among the best basketball players in East Texas, but All East Texas basketball teams were not selected in those years. He scored about 500 points, averaging nearly 20 points-per-game, during his senior basketball season, giving him a career total of approximately 1,800 points and making him White Oak's all-time leader in career points by about 300 points (information given to him several years later by then White Oak basketball coach, Bob Proctor). During most of the basketball games his senior year, he was continuously double-teamed, and White Oak's other "big" guys did not help much with the scoring and rebounding against good competition, although the Roughnecks still managed to win the district championship. They lost in bi-district to Paul Pewit, who went on to win the Class A state championship.

A few weeks after basketball season ended, David was at home watching TV while eating supper. The All State basketball teams were announced on a local TV station sports show, and David saw that he was selected for the Class A first-team All State. He was very pleased but did not realize that he had just become part of the historical record for White Oak and Gregg County mentioned above.

Later that spring David was told that he had received Honorable Mention All American in basketball and had also been designated as a top college basketball recruit by a national magazine.

During his senior track season, David was among the fastest 100-yard dash sprinters in East Texas, losing only once in invitational meets in which he competed against all classifications. At the Gladewater Invitational, a highly publicized showdown occurred between him and best friend-cousin Tommy Minter of Gladewater. At the end of the race, David was picked by the first-place picker and by the second-place picker, the latter from Gladewater. Both pickers insisted they were correct. Of course, Minter was the other runner in question. After several minutes of debate between the officials, David suggested that they call it a tie. The officials decided to flip for the first place metal, and Minter won the flip. It was then announced that Minter had won the race (probably because he had won the flip). Bailey Marshall, White Oak's coach loudly protested, "Wait a minute. We agreed to call it a tie. The coin flip was just for the metal!" Then the announcer said, "Actually we have a tie for first place between Minter and Alexander." A new record of 9.8 was set, but a year later only Minter's name was listed as the record holder. However, a few years later the Minter-Alexander record was broken by a Spring Hill sprinter.

David won the 100 at the district and regional meets, and placed second at the state meet. He was picked first but then awarded second based on the photo finish. However, that state meet turned out to be one of David's best individual performances in his athletic career. He got the baton in 5th place in the sprint relay and anchored the team to victory. He then got the baton in 7th place in the mile relay and made up about 30 yards not only to win the race but also to assure the team state championship for White Oak. He ran almost two seconds faster than he had ever run before in anchoring the mile relay. White Oak scored 40 points in winning the state meet. Their coach later emphasized that without David's contributions, they would have probably scored only 2-3 points that day.

Five months earlier White Oak's football team had tied Mart in the state championship game and were declared co-state champs. In those years overtime was not part of high school football. If a state championship game was tied at the end of regulation, the two teams were declared co-champions. With about three minutes left in the fourth quarter, David attempted a 40-yard field goal (only his second attempt in his entire career). A 25 MPH cross-wind pushed the ball about a foot outside the right upright. Otherwise, the Roughnecks would have had an outright state championship instead of a co-state championship.

Although some say that the fall of 1957 team is not among White Oak's best ever football teams, it's the only White Oak football team ever to make it to a state championship game. The Roughnecks of 1957 lost their first game to Class 2A powerhouse (in those years), New London, but did not lose again, ending with a 12-1-2 record. They also played to a 6-6 tie against highly-favored Sundown from far West Texas, but won on penetrations to advance to the championship game. White Oak also was a big underdog in their regional match with Wilmer Hutchins from the Dallas area, who supposedly had two of the best athletes in the state, a QB and a runningback. The Dallas News stated the day of the game that "Wilmer Hutchins runs the option like they thought of it first." The day after White Oak beat them by about 40 points, the Dallas News stated that "Wilmer Hutchins ran the option like they'd never thought of it before." In the quarterfinal game against Albany, White Oak won in the mud by about 20 points, and David averaged 63 yards on three punts, reportedly a Class A record at the time.

David was among eight stars from that 1957 team selected to White Oak's All Century Football Team, five of whom were also selected All State, and six played college football. So that co-state championship team might have been better than some thought or remember.

David had another impressive receiving yardage season, pushing his career total to approximately 2,000 yards, a record no other Roughneck has ever come close to matching. This record was achieved even though White Oak seldom threw the ball more that ten times a game during those years. Many of today's teams average 30-40 passes per game. David's average per catch was probably 20+ yards.

1.2.7 Gregg County Outstanding All Round High School Athlete

For reasons indicated in the above sections, David was selected as Gregg County Outstanding All Round High School Athlete during the summer after his senior year. A large lighted picture of him in his basketball uniform was displayed at the Gregg County Fair the following fall. The picture was later given to David as a keepsake and was hung in his Space-Sports-Music Room in his home with the following wording: "For honors and accomplishments during his four-year varsity career at White Oak High School, including starring on state championship teams in each football, basketball, and track, being the only White Oak and Gregg County athlete ever selected first-team All State in both football and basketball, being selected for both the Texas Coaches' All Star football and basketball games, and for setting school records in each football, basketball, track, and baseball."

1.2.8 First Recipient of the Joe Roughneck Award

The Joe Roughneck Award was first awarded in 1958 (David's senior year), and David was the recipient. The award has been presented every year since to an outstanding all-round athlete who has brought special honor to White Oak through both sports and leadership contributions. Back 25-30 years ago, they began giving this award to each a male and a female athlete.

1.2.9 Texas High School Coaches' Association (THSCA) All Star Selection in Both Football and Basketball

David was selected as a THSCA All Star (North Team) for both football and basketball. Because he could not play on both teams, as the games were scheduled the same week as part of the THSCA Coaching School, David chose to play in the football game. The Coaching School that summer of 1958 was held in Houston, and the All Star football game was played in Rice Stadium. David reported on a Sunday weighing about 185. Because of the Houston heat and humidity, to which he was unaccustomed, by game time the following Saturday evening, he weighed about 170. He was a starting end and was among the fastest 3-4 players on the field that evening. On the first play from scrimmage, he got 10 yards behind the South's secondary, but Sonny Gibbs, the North QB (and later starter at TCU), threw a shot just beyond David's fingertips. Had he put a little air under the pass, they would have had an easy touchdown. David got only one other pass thrown to him the entire game, and it was almost intercepted. He did make several key blocks, and the North won in a close game.

One day between lunch and the evening practice, David decided to go downtown Houston to see his girlfriend, Cherry, who just happened to be the daughter of David's high school basketball coach, Emil Hanicak. It was 3-4 miles from Rice University to downtown, so country-boy David got out on Main Street to thumb a ride. A big fancy limo pulled up and the driver asked David where he was headed. When David told him, the driver told David to get in. David and the nice old gentleman in the back of the limo talked all the way to downtown. Then the limo stopped to let the old gentleman out, and he told the driver to take David on to the Rice Hotel, where Cherry and her family were staying. On the way to the Rice Hotel, David asked the driver who the old gentleman was. The Driver replied that he was Mr. Battlestein, owner of the Battlestein department stores and one of the richest men in the Southwest at that time.

1.2.10 White Oak's Super Sports Era of the Late-1950's

David was one of 7-8 exceptional all-round White Oak athletes in the late-1950's that led in the accomplishment of what is often referred to as the Super Sports Era of the Late-1950's. In a 14-month period from March of 1957 to May of 1958, White Oak won state championships in four different sports—basketball in March of 1957, girls' doubles in tennis in May of 1957, football (co-championship) in December of 1957, and track in May of 1958. White Oak has won eight team state championships in its entire history, and four of them were won during this 14-month Super Sports Era. David started and starred on three of these state championship teams (basketball, football, and track). Teammate-classmate Bob Wayt also started and starred on these three championship teams, and he and David are reportedly the only Texas high school athletes ever to "start" on state championship teams in these three sports. In the mid-1950's Abilene High School won state championships in football, basketball, and baseball in a 2-year period (that is, with the same athletes involved), and they are reportedly the only high school ever to do that. But only White Oak has ever won state champion-ships in football, basketball, and track in a 2-year period with the same athletes involved. White Oak also placed third in basketball at the state tournament in spring of 1959 and had what many believe was one of the best football teams in White Oak's history in the fall of 1958, but that football team was disqualified from the playoffs because of an ineligible (too-old) player. During the three full years of this Super Sports Era (from the fall of 1956 through the spring of 1959), the White Oak boys won 14 of 15 district championships in the combo of foot-ball, basketball, baseball, track, and tennis, losing only in baseball in 1957 by one run in the game that decided the district championship.

When White Oak's All Century Teams for football and basketball were selected in 2000, 90 were selected to the football team and 19 to the basketball team. Only seven athletes were selected to both the football and basketball teams, and five of those seven were from the Super Sports Era of the Late-1950's. They were David and Bob (Class of 1958), Mike Cobb (Class of 1957), Jim Cox (Class of 1959), and Russell Wayt (Class of 1961, who started in football and basketball as a sophomore in 1959, and then became one of White Oak's great all-round athletes during the next two years).

Some might say that this super sports era occurred back when White Oak was a Class A high school and therefore should not be considered such a big deal. They might add that the talent and competition back then don't compare with that of recent years. However, most who really understand sports would agree that the merits of sports feats and honors are a relative thing. Athletes today are bigger and faster and more skillful overall, and that trend will likely continue into the future. But most of the great athletes of 40-60 years ago would still be very good today if their youth could be restored and they were given today's facilities and equipment. Relatively few athletes in White Oak's history have had the all-round size, skill, and speed combination of 5-6 of the athletes in the late-1950's. Relative to the overall school populations and classifications today compared to the late-1950's, White Oak is essentially at the same relative position today in Class 3A as in the late-1950's as a Class A high school. State championships and All State selections and (especially) All Star selections are rare in any era and at any classification. For White Oak to have won four state championships and to have had, combining football and basketball, twelve All State selections and five All Star selections (Cobb and Alexander each were selected as both football and basketball All Stars) during this Super Sports Era should be considered truly out-standing by all.

1.2.11 College Recruitment

David was recruited by about 20 major universities, including all of the former Southwest Conference schools, plus several other major college teams such as Oklahoma, LSU, Alabama, Penn State, Army, Navy, Air Force, plus many smaller universities. All of them offered David full football scholarships but several of them also offered him full scholarships in basketball and track. Legendary football coaches such as Darrell Royal (Texas), Jess Neely (Rice), and Abe Martin (TCU) came to White Oak to David's home to try to convince him to sign with their programs. David chose Baylor because of about four factors: (1) cousin and best friend Tommy Minter committed to Baylor, and David and Tommy wanted to be college teammates and roommates, (2) Baylor offered David full scholarships in each football, basketball, and track, (3) Baylor track coach, Jack Patterson, impressed David a great deal, and (4) several other football blue chippers, such as Ronny Bull from Bishop and Bobby Ply from Mission, had committed to Baylor.

In those years, a high school athlete was not allowed to visit a college campus on a recruiting trip for any given sport until he was completely finished with all high school sports. David was not finished with baseball until late-May, so he had to limit his recruiting trips to only 5-6 universities. He visited Texas, TCU, Texas Tech, Rice, and A&M in addition to Baylor. Texas was too big, TCU too dull, Rice discouraged him from majoring in math or science, a sand storm hit while he was visiting Texas Tech, and he was turned off by the shaved heads (freshmen) and lack of females at A&M back then. Baylor turned out to be the best choice for him then and in the long run. Although Baylor's football program has been down in recent years, other programs such as boys' tennis and girls' basketball (each in which Baylor has won national championships) and track and baseball have been very good, and David is proud to be a Baylor Bear.

1.2.12 College Football

When David attended Baylor, freshmen were not eligible to play on the varsity but had a separate freshmen team that played 6-7 games. College rules then required a one-platoon system, which meant everyone played both offense and defense. David was a starting wide receiver and cornerback on a freshmen team that included future All American runningback Ronny Bull, future NCAA passing champ Ronnie Stanley, and other future pro football players Tommy Minter and Bobby Ply. David led the team in receiving and was selected second-team All

Southwest Conference Freshmen Team. The first-team wide receiver was Arkansas' Lance Alsworth, later an All Pro receiver. David also punted for the freshmen team.

David says the worst part of that freshmen football season was when the freshmen scrimmaged against the varsity during practice. The varsity fullback was senior 230-pound Larry Hickman, one of the biggest fullbacks in college football at that time. As a cornerback, David at 180 pounds had to tackle Larry in the open field several times. David says that usually he couldn't figure out where he was for several seconds after such tackles.

David had noticed for 2-3 years that he did not have good stamina. It was as if he just couldn't get into good shape. He had noticed the stamina problem particularly in track while in high school. He began anchoring the mile relay as a high school sophomore and almost always got sick and had chest discomfort after the race. By the beginning of his sophomore year in college, his lack of stamina became more apparent in football. After running 2-3 long pass patterns, he would become dizzy and sometimes nauseated. After briefly passing out during wind sprints at the end of a practice early during his sophomore year, he was called in to talk to the coaching staff. David agreed to redshirt and try to get in better condition. After several weeks as a redshirt, things didn't improve. He talked with Coach Jack "Pat" Patterson, who encouraged him to switch to a full track scholarship for at least a year. Although head football coach John Bridgers tried to persuade David several times during the next year or so to return to football at least as a punter, David chose to compete only in track during the remainder of his college career. However, in the spring of his senior year, David was asked by the athletic department's public affairs director if he had any interest in playing pro football. The American Football League was brand new, and their teams were prepared to draft about anyone who might have potential to play in their league. They were apparently interested in David because of his speed and punting ability even though he had not played varsity football. David had already accepted a job with the Department of Defense, and although he sent word that he was not interested in trying out for pro football, he was later told that he had been drafted in the late rounds by the Dallas Texans (who later became the Kansas City Chiefs) of the American Football League and by the Los Angeles Rams (who later became the St. Louis Rams) of the National Football League.

1.2.13 College Track

David's freshmen class included 5-6 track athletes who were among the fastest in Baylor's history to that time. David was about the fifth fastest among these freshmen and there had been probably only 4-5 in early years that had been faster than David. As in football, freshmen were not eligible to participate with the varsity but had a separate freshmen track team. Early in the season, Coach Pat had the seven freshmen sprinters run a 100-yard dash to determine who would be on the sprint (440) relay team. David with a time of 9.75 placed fifth behind Ray Knaub, Roy Smalley, Tommy Minter, and Ronny Bull. However, Ronny, who later became an All American runningback and the NFL's Rookie of the Year, suffered a serious pulled muscle a short time later and decided not to run track, and David became the fourth man (second leg) on the sprint relay. That freshmen sprint relay team won every race they entered and set freshmen records at nearly every meet in which they participated, including the NCAA freshmen record at the time. David also ran on the mile and 880 relay teams that also won nearly every race they ran, and they set Baylor freshmen records in all of these relays.

At the beginning of his sophomore year, David was the "fifth" man on the sprint, 880, and mile relays, but he ran on all three of the relays the majority of the time because one of the top four runners was either injured or entered in other events to earn more team points. David ran on both the mile and 880 relay teams that year when they set Baylor varsity records at the time. The sprint relay that year won 12 of 14 races while participating in some of the major meets in the nation, and they ran on national TV several times. A big disappointment for David that sophomore year was that he pulled a hamstring about two weeks prior to the Southwest Conference Meet. The 1960 Bears won Baylor's first ever conference championship in track, outpointing a highly-favored Texas team by about 15 points. It was still a great time for David even though he was not able to participate.

Captain Billy Hollis was the only senior sprinter on the 1960 team, and 9.5-sprinter Ray Knaub, who had grown up in Nebraska, decided to transfer to the University of Nebraska to begin his junior year. However, two very fast sophomore sprinters, Bill Kemp and Glynn Fields, joined the varsity in 1961. David therefore remained the #5 guy on both the sprint and 880 relays, but continued to run both relays most of the time because of injuries and such. However, David stopped running the mile relay because he just could not finish strongly or improve his time. Sixteen years later, when his abnormal coronary system was discovered along with his coronary disease, there was finally an explanation for the stamina problems that had plagued him throughout high school and college.

Baylor had another impressive season in 1961 in the national invitational meets, but Texas defeated Baylor in the Southwest Conference Meet at Rice by about five points. Texas' best sprinter edged Baylor's best sprinters in both the 100 and 220, and that proved to be the difference. David just missed placing in the 220.

In 1962, David's senior year, Baylor's relay teams were again among the best in the nation, winning or placing high in a majority of the races they entered. The major invitational meets during those years, such as Drake and Kansas, gave watches for first place in each event. David accumulated several of these watches during his varsity years and gave a couple of them to his dad, who wore the faces off them.

At the Texas Relays in 1962, David was just returning to full speed following another hamstring injury, but Coach Pat decided to run David as the second leg of the sprint relay. David overheard the team trainer say that Baylor could not win the sprint relay with David running on it. David proceeded to gain about five yards on the field, and Baylor won the race by 5-6 yards. This became one of David's more satisfying college track memories.

At the 1962 conference meet, held at Baylor's brand new track and field complex, David finished his track career in good style. He finished fifth in the 220 and started the winning 440 relay. Roy Smalley, who usually started the 440 relay, switched places with David because Roy had a sore hamstring. As famous starter Mule Frazier called, "Get set," Sandy, who had come down to the fence about 20 yards from the start, screamed, "Come on, David!" Instead of shooting the gun, Mule told the runners to come up. Before he went back to his blocks, David went over to Sandy and told her that she needed to keep quiet during the start. David glanced over at Mule as he headed back to his blocks, and Mule had a big smile on his face. Teammates Kemp and Fields place 1st and 2nd in both the 100 and 220 and ran on both of the winning relays. Smalley won the 440 and anchored the mile relay. Several other Bears, in addition to David, scored unexpected points in one of the greatest team efforts in Baylor's track history. Baylor was again a 20-point underdog to Texas but defeated the Longhorns by about 20 points. At the end of the meet, Coach Pat was so overcome with emotion that he could not talk. David and hurdler David Bennett put Coach Pat on their shoulders and carried him across the infield as the Baylor fans cheered wildly. David's dad was waiting at the gate, and he greeted David with, "Well, Son, you saved the best till last."

1.2.13.1 Racing Against Olympic Champions

At the West Texas Relays in Odessa in April of 1960, two of the best quarter-milers in the world, Glen Davis and Mike Larabee, were invited to run an exhibition 400-meter race. They were just beginning to train for the 1960 Olympics scheduled in August. They requested that a runner be put 2-3 lanes to their outside to serve as a "rabbit." The head official asked Coach Pat if he had someone who could be the "rabbit." Coach Pat volunteered David and told him he could drop out at about 300 meters if he wanted to. Davis and Larabee lined up in lanes 3 and 4, and they put David out in lane 6. At 300 meters David still could not see or hear them, so he continued to run. With about 40 meters remaining, they still were not in David's sight. Then with about 15 meters remaining, they edged ahead of David and finished in a tie about a half stride ahead of David. Afterward they laughingly told David that he had "scared the hell out of them" and how embarrassed they would have been had they not beat him. David got their autographs, a pair of nice cuff links for placing "third," and a great lifetime memory. At the Olympics in August, Davis and Larabee both placed in the 400 meters and both ran on the winning 1600-meter relay team.

David ran against the great Bob Hayes in a 100-yard dash preliminary at the 1962 Drake relays. He tells folks, "I once ran against Bob Hayes and beat him for 70 yards. Unfortunately, we were running 100 yards. Truth is, he was just playing with us." Hayes later set the world's record in the 100-yard dash, won the 100-meter dash and anchored the winning 400-meter relay in the Olympics, and was an All Pro receiver for the Dallas Cowboys.

1.2.14 Post-College Sports Activities

David played in the NASA leagues in basketball and slow-pitch softball during his first 3-4 years there, and his teams won the championships nearly every year. David was the leading scorer in basketball and hit a home run about every 2 or 3 times at-bats in softball. Although there were few great athletes among the NASA engineers and scientists, David's teams usually included 3-4 other good athletes.

In the basketball playoffs in 1966, David badly tore a calf muscle and was never able to play at full speed again. However, in 1968 his former team got to the playoffs but had three players out for the championship game because of illness or out-of-town duty. They asked David if he would suit up and maybe substitute for a few minutes if needed. In the fourth quarter, David played about three minutes and scored six points, and his team won the championship by about that margin.

David also began playing golf and tennis fairly regularly after he began working at NASA. Although he never took any lessons in either, he was a consistent "bogey" golfer and a relatively good tennis player in doubles. Because of his weak backhand, he was only a mediocre singles player. After his heart surgery in the late-1970's, he essentially gave up golf, but he continued to play tennis doubles periodically for several more years until arthritis and heart disease prohibited his movement and stamina. He also enjoyed bowling for several years and usually carried an average of about 165. He has remained an avid sports fan, especially of high school and college sports. He still attends quite a few White Oak games in all sports (including girls sports) and often sends notes of congratulations and encouragement to the players and coaches. He enjoys watching professional sports on TV but has not attended a pro game live in many years. He believes the players are way overpaid relative to their contribution to society.

In the spring of 2007 David was honored to be invited to throw the first pitch for the annual game between the White Oak baseball alumni and the current high school team. The "first-pitch" ball was later autographed by all of the players and presented to David for a keepsake.

1.2.15 Major Sports Honors and Achievements Summary

1.2.15.1 High School (White Oak, 1954-1958):

Multi-Sport:

* Started on State Championship Teams in each football, basketball, and track
* Invited to play in the Texas High School Coaches All Star Game in both
        football and basketball; played in football game
* Made AP <u>first-team</u> All State in both football and basketball
* Made All District three years in each football, basketball, and baseball
* Earned 16 varsity letters, four in each football, basketball, baseball, and track
* Gregg County Outstanding All Round High School Athlete
* First Joe Roughneck Award recipient

Football (end/receiver, safety, punt and kick-off returns, punter, place kicker):

* Captain of Co-State Championship Team
* THSCA All Star (North)
* AP First-Team All State 2 years (unanimous choice senior year)
* All East Texas 2 years
* All District 3 years
* White Oak's All Century Team
* Starter 3 years
* Lettered 4 years
* School record still held: career pass receiving yardage (~2,000 yards)
* Probably school record for career passes caught and career touchdowns
        by a receiver

Basketball (center/forward):

* Leading scorer on State Championship Team
* THSCA All Star Invitation (North)
* AP First-Team All State (1958) and Honorable Mention All State (1957)
* First-Team State Tournament All Tournament Team (1957)
* Captain
* All District 3 years
* White Oak's All Century Team
* Lettered and started 4 years
* School record still held: career points (~1,800)
* Probably school record for career free throws made and career free
        throw percentage
* Personal Best: 167 free throws without missing at about age 50

Track (100, 220, sprint and mile relays):

* Starred as high-point man on State Championship Team
* Placed second in 100 at state meet
* Anchored three state championship relay teams
* Won total of five state meet metals during career
* Won 100 at district and regional meets 3 years
* Won 220 at district meet as a freshman on the varsity
* Lettered 4 years
* School record still held: 100-yard dash (9.7)

Baseball (centerfielder, pitcher):

* All East Texas
* All District 3 years
* Lettered and started 4 years
* School record still held: single season batting average (565), probably career batting average (~400)

1.2.15.2 College (Baylor, 1958-1962):

Multi-Sport:

* One of few Baylor recruits ever offered full scholarships in each football, basketball, and track

Track:

* Member of two Outdoor Track & Field (Southwest) Conference Championship Teams (sprints and relays); Baylor has had only three such conference championship teams in her entire history, and no trackman has ever run on more than two of them
* On relay teams that won or placed high at major meets across the nation
* Ran on national TV several times
* Individually ran against Olympic champions on two occasions
* Three varsity letters, one freshmen letter
* Chosen to deliver dedication speech for Coach Patterson's honorary bust in spring of 2005
* Selected to Baylor Letterwinners' Wall of Honor in the fall of 2005, and afterward was introduced on national TV and was honorary rider in homecoming parade

Football:

* Leading receiver on freshmen team that included four eventual pro football players
* Second-Team All Southwest Conference Freshmen Team
* Freshmen letter and starter
* Drafted in the late rounds by both the National and American Football Leagues

1.2.15.3 Summer Baseball (Little League through American Legion)

* All Star Team and top hitter (batting average) each of these six summer baseball years except as an 11-year-old Little Leaguer
* Hit first home run in the history of Longview Little League Baseball as an 11 year old

1.2.16 Sports Records

1.2.16.1 White Oak High School Sports Records Reportedly Still Held

Multi-Sport:

* One of only two Texas high school athletes ever to "start" on State Championship Teams in each football, basketball, and track (the other athlete was teammate-classmate Bob Wayt)
* One of only three Roughnecks ever invited to play in the Texas High School Coaches All Star Game in both football and basketball (the other two were Mike Cobb and Russell Wayt)
* Only Roughneck ever to make <u>first-team</u> All State in both football and basketball (reportedly also the only one ever to do so from any Gregg County high school, and one of the relatively few ever to do so in Texas schoolboy history)
* Only Roughneck ever to make All District three years each in football, basketball, and baseball
* Only male Roughneck ever to earn 16 varsity letters, four in each football, basketball, baseball, and track (was a starter all four years in basketball, baseball, and track, and started three years in football)

Football:

* Only Roughneck ever to make <u>first-team</u> All State two different years (was an end/receiver)
* Career receiving yardage: ~2,000 yards (approximately 700 yards more than second best)

Basketball:

* Career scoring: ~1,800 points (approximately 300 more than second best; was a center/forward)

Baseball:

* Single-season batting average: 565 in 1956, when selected as first-team center-fielder to multi-class Greater Tyler-Longview All East Texas Baseball Team (four-year career batting average was approximately 400, which may also still be a school record)

Track:

* 100-yard dash: 9.7 (still school record when switched to meters; a 9.7 100-yard dash is equivalent to about a 10.5 100-meter dash, which would be faster than the standing school record in the 100-meter dash)
* Only Roughneck ever to run on (anchor) three State Championship relays (mile relay in 1957 and 1958, sprint relay in 1958)
* Only Roughneck ever to place in the 100-yard dash at State Meet (placed second in 1958)
* Only Roughneck ever to win five State Meet metals: three gold and one silver (see above) and one bronze (1955 sprint relay as a freshman)
* Only Roughneck ever to win three individual track events at Regional Meet (100-yard dash in 1956, 1957, and 1958)

1.2.16.2 Baylor Sports Records David Helped Set

Track:

* Varsity mile relay
* Freshmen mile relay
* Freshmen sprint relay (also Texas Relays and NCAA freshman records)

1.2.17 Fondest Sports Memories

The following is a quick summary of David's fondest sports memories listed in chronological order.

* Hitting the first home run in the history of Longview Little League Baseball

* Making two free throws in the last few seconds to win by one point his first ever
   junior high basketball game
* Being the leading scorer on White Oak's 1957 State Championship basketball
   team
* Being a captain of White Oak's 1957 Co-State Championship football team
* Being selected unanimous first-team All State in football after his senior season
* Leading White Oak to State Championship in track in 1958, involving proba-
   bly his best individual performance of his entire sports career
* Being selected as 1958 Gregg County Outstanding All Round High School
   Athlete
* Being selected first-team All State in basketball after his senior season, making
   him the only White Oak and Gregg County athlete ever selected first-team
   All State in both football and basketball (and one of the few in Texas
   schoolboy history)
* Being selected Honorable Mention High School All American in basketball in
   1958
* Playing in the Texas High School Coaches' Association's All Star football game,
   after also being selected for the All Star basketball game
* Being part of two of the three outdoor track & field conference championship
   track teams in Baylor's history, especially the 1962 championship team
* Running against three eventual Olympic champions, Bob Hayes (100 and
   4X100), Glen Davis (400 and 4X400), and Mike Larabee (4X400)
* Delivering dedication speech for Coach Patterson's honorary bust at Baylor's
   Hart-Patterson Track Complex, and being on program with Olympic
   champion Michael Johnson and Olympic-Baylor coach Clyde Hart
* Being selected and inducted to Baylor Letterwinners' Wall of Honor, and afterward being introduced on national TV and being an honorary rider in the
   homecoming parade the next fall

1.3 SPACE CAREER

1.3.1 Background

David had no idea while growing up in the 1950's that he would end up having a
career in aerospace. Back then, people who suggested it was possible to send men
to the Moon were considered weird by most. Even David's dad often said, "If
God had wanted man on the Moon, He would have Put him there Himself."

Can you imagine George's surprise when his own son helped put men on the Moon? In high school David especially liked math and science and majored in math-physics in college, but throughout high school and most of college he basically planned to be a high school math-science teacher and probably a coach.

1.3.2 First Full-Fledged Job

NASA had not begun hiring from Texas universities like Baylor prior to David's graduation in the spring of 1962, although they had begun constructing the Manned Spacecraft Center (later named the Johnson Space Center) between Houston and Galveston. David accepted a job with the Department of Defense's Naval Ordnance Lab in Corona, California (NOLC), which was mainly involved with missile warhead research. He began there in June of 1962, sharing an apartment with Bob Kehl, also a Baylor grad who had started to work at NOLC a couple of weeks earlier. David had worked every summer since his sophomore year in high school (at White Oak Schools, for a company clearing utility right-of-ways, and for the State of Texas measuring cotton acreage in Gregg County), but the job at NOLC was his first full-fledged job.

1.3.3 The Beginning and Early Years at NASA

David earned enough leave and money to fly back to White Oak from California for the 1962 Christmas holidays. He and Sandy had become engaged in August when she came to Corona with his family. They had set their wedding date for mid-February of 1963, but expected to begin their life together in California. David returned to Corona on a Sunday evening in early-January and found out that Kehl and another Baylor friend at NOLC, Leroy Hall, had gone to Houston during the holidays and hired on with NASA. The next morning David called the Personnel Office at the Manned Spacecraft Center and asked about applying for a job. He was told to send his college transcript, which he immediately did. A few days later NASA called back and offered David a job, and he chose the first Monday in February as his starting date. Of course, he and Sandy were very happy that they would be living in the Houston area, about 200 miles from home instead of over 1,500 miles away in Corona. David moved back to White Oak a week or so prior to reporting to NASA so that he and Sandy could buy some furniture together and go to Houston and find a place to live. On this quick trip to Houston, they stayed with Paula and Tommy Jankowski, who were among their dearest friends through the years.

During David's first day at work, he was given a choice between joining the orbital mechanics/rendezvous analysis work and a couple of other areas of work. He fortunately chose the former and became one of the top rendezvous specialists. His first major accomplishment was the development of a rendezvous algorithm/routine called the "conic fit" routine. It was first used in Gemini and then for the Apollo rendezvous around the Moon.

During David's first week at work, he asked his immediate boss, Bill Tindall, if he could have a week of advanced leave to get married and honeymoon. Bill seemed a bit surprised at the bold request, but agreed to it. Years later when David became part of Bill's staff at the Center's highest level (directorate), Bill told David that he considered firing him when he asked for the advanced leave after only 2-3 days on the job. He said he figured that David was either nuts or very gutsy and confident, and that he had obviously made the right decision.

1.3.4 Apollo 1 Disaster

The most terrible thing to happen during the early years was the Apollo 1 fire on the ground during a simulation that claimed the lives of three of our great astronauts, Gus Grissom, Ed White, and Roger Chaffee. NASA originally had an high-oxygen-content atmosphere inside the Apollo cabin. During the simulation, a spark set off the fire which (because of the high oxygen content) spread instantly throughout the cabin. The astronauts were probably dead in a 20-30 seconds, although they tried desperately to open the hatch. Most of the next year or so was spent changing the cabin atmosphere to a nearly-normal air contents and redesigning the hatch such that it could be opened from the inside in just a few seconds.

1.3.5 Football Rendezvous

By the mid-1960's David was involved in designing both the nominal (desired) and contingency rendezvous plans and techniques for the Apollo missions. The first manned Apollo mission was Apollo 7, which flew in Earth orbit with the objective of basically checking out the spacecraft's systems. Then Apollo 8 was sent out around the Moon, and nearly everyone who was then in school or older probably remembers that the astronauts read scriptures on the way back to Earth. The first rendezvous mission was Apollo 9, an Earth-orbit mission with the objective of checking out the Lunar Module (LM) systems. To accomplish this, the LM was separated from the Command Service Module (CSM) and maneuvered into an orbit such that the two spacecraft would get about 100 miles apart but automatically come back into close proximity without an additional maneuver (burn). The motion of the LM trajectory relative to the CSM (as if the CSM were stationary) looked a lot like a football. Being a former football player, David named the rendezvous plan the "football rendezvous." Soon the other flight planners, the flight controllers, and even the astronauts were referring to the Apollo 9 rendezvous as the "football rendezvous."

1.3.6 Apollo Lunar Rendezvous Plans and Support

David and a few other mission planners worked directly with the Apollo 11 (first lunar landing mission) astronauts, Neil Armstrong, Buzz Aldrin, and Mike Collins, to design the rendezvous required in lunar orbit for the Moon landing missions. After the landing and stay on the Moon, the ascent stage of the LM launched back into lunar orbit, using the descent stage as a launch pad. Through a series of maneuvers, a rendezvous was effected with the CSM, which had remained in lunar orbit. David and Buzz named the maneuvers and did most of the detailed designing for this plan. David says that Buzz was probably a genius, although all of the astronauts were very smart.

As a point of clarification, the difference between rendezvous and docking is as follows. Rendezvous begins when the two spacecraft are far apart, sometimes thousands of miles apart. Several targeted rendezvous maneuvers (orbital changes) are usually required to bring the two spacecraft into close proximity (within 50 feet or so). Then the docking procedure, which connects the two spacecraft using docking hardware, begins.

David helped educate all of the Apollo astronauts about the rendezvous plans. He also supported the operations during the actual missions (real time) as part of the staff support team in Houston's Mission Control Center.

1.3.7 Apollo 11 Critical Decision and Close Call

When the LM landed that first time on the lunar surface, one of its feet landed in a slight depression, causing the LM to tilt slightly in that direction. The exact consistency of the lunar surface was not known. If the LM had continued to tilt, there could have been problems with the launch back into orbit. David and his rendezvous position partner, Ken Young, had only 10-15 seconds to recommend whether the LM (ascent stage) should immediately begin an ascent back into orbit or stay on the surface. The telemetry indicated that the LM was becoming stable, and David and Ken knew that Neil and Buzz would desire to stretch the limits as far as possible, so they nervously gave a "Go" to stay. Hopefully, the rest of the story is known by all—a successful mission watched around the world and still considered by most as one of the greatest technical moments and feats in the history of mankind.

The actual landing itself almost didn't happen. Neil kept looking for a smoother spot to land, and almost ran out of fuel in the descent engine. When the Eagle landed, there was only 10 seconds of fuel remaining. Had he hovered 10 seconds more, either the landing would have been aborted or the Eagle probably would have crashed.

1.3.8 Apollo 10 Fun

Apollo 10 went to the Moon a few months before Apollo 11, but on Apollo 10 we did not plan to land on the Moon. The objective was to test all the systems in lunar orbit, including the LM maneuvering systems. Because there would not be a landing, the rendezvous maneuvers, approach, lighting, etc., would be different than those for a landing mission. A few days prior to the mission, the astronauts became concerned about the rendezvous plans, especially the abort and rescue plans that could be required should something go wrong. They called one morning and asked the rendezvous specialists to come to the Kennedy Space Center and brief them. David and a couple of others jumped on a plane and got there about 4 p. m., but the astronauts did not finish in the training simulators until about 7 p. m. Then they said they were tired and wanted to eat dinner first. So they all went to the astronauts' quarters and had big steaks and all the trimmings, and it was about 10 p. m. before David started his briefing. About five minutes into the briefing, he began to hear some loud snoring. John Young, the CSM pilot, had dozed off. Tom Stafford, the mission commander, elbowed John and said, "John, wake up! If something goes wrong, you may need to come rescue us." John replied, "Man, I'm so tired I'm not sure I can stay awake. If we have a problem up there, Houston will tell me what to do." Gene Cernan, the LM pilot, grabbed a pitcher of water and threatened to pour it over John's head if he didn't stay awake. David wasn't sure what to do but continued his briefing, and John stayed awake, or at least he didn't start snoring again.

The mission launched a few days later, and everything went pretty much as planned. However, when they started the descent engine to start back up (instead of landing), it appeared that they were still heading toward the surface of the Moon because they had failed to reset one of the displays. Gene Cernan shouted out, "Son of a bitch!" Mission Control quickly cut the sound to the TV networks and had a private talk with Gene. A few weeks later, David went to North American in Los Angeles to give a briefing on the Apollo 11 rendezvous plan. Afterward, he joined a bunch of people gathered to see and hear the Apollo 10 astronauts, who were there on their "at-a-boy" tour. Near the end of Stafford's speech, he said, "By the way, we apparently nicked the padding in the tunnel when we crawled from the CSM into the LM. A bunch of itchy stuff got into the air and then somehow got into our suits." Of course, he was making up all of this. Then he added, "At one point it got so bad that, well, you may remember Gene shouting out, 'Some of us itch!'"

Tom Staffard did not fly again on Apollo, but he flew on the Apollo-Soyuz Test Project, the Earth-orbit rendezvous mission with the Soviets in the mid-1970's. Gene Cernan later flew on Apollo 17 as the mission commander and has the distinction of being the last man on the Moon (to date). John Young later flew on Apollo 16 as the mission commander and also flew the first Shuttle orbital flight.

For each of the Apollo landing missions, except for Apollo 10, after the LM ascent stage launched from the Moon, performed the rendezvous and docking with the CSM, and the LM astronauts transferred back into the Command Module, the LM was separated from the CSM and temporarily left in lunar orbit. Then after the CSM headed back toward Earth, the LM was maneuvered remotely and crashed into the Moon. For Apollo 10, however, the LM was left in lunar orbit because there was not yet an instrument on the lunar surface to measure the shock waves that would be caused by such a crash. David was stopped by a Houston Chronicle reporter outside the Control Center a few days after Apollo 10 and asked if later Apollo missions might collide with the Apollo 10 LM while in orbit around the Moon. David explained that such a collision was not impossible but that the odds were essentially zero, like one in several million, and he explained why in detail. The next day a headline on the front page of the Chronicle read, "Debris Problem Exists for Apollo 11" and the article began, "NASA mission designer, David Alexander, says there is a chance that the Apollo 11 spacecraft could collide with the Apollo 10 Lunar Module earlier left in lunar orbit." David was quite upset with the article and the reporter. Of course, there was nothing close to a collision on Apollo 11 or any of the later Apollo missions. The powerless Apollo 10 Lunar Module may still be orbiting around the Moon.

1.3.9 Apollo 13: A Near Disaster

As the Apollo 13 movie portrayed, we were very fortunate to get our astronauts back alive. David was involved in designing the correction maneuver needed to assure that the spacecraft would enter the Earth's atmosphere at an acceptable angle. The trajectory that sent the spacecraft to the Moon (for all the Apollo lunar missions) was designed to come back safely to Earth without any additional maneuvering being required, in case something happened to prevent the spacecraft from doing a maneuver. However, because of the explosion on Apollo 13 on the way to the Moon, the trajectory was thrown off enough to make a correction maneuver necessary. The correction maneuver had to be made using the descent stage engine, and the attitude had to be controlled manually, a combination that had never been simulated or even thought of. There were a couple of other things that had to be accomplished that also had never been thought of before. The filter to absorb the excess carbon dioxide—because three astronauts (instead of two) were forced to live in the LM for several days—had to be constructed using materials already onboard the spacecraft, and a new method to re-power-up the Command Module prior to entry into the Earth's atmosphere using minimum power had to be developed in the ground simulators. The odds of all of these things working were not good, but somehow they worked, and we got our guys back alive. In the opinion of many NASA people, including David, the safe return of the Apollo 13 astronauts was truly a miracle. As stated by Apollo flight director and NASA legend Gene Kranz, "Apollo 13 was considered a failure by some, but by those who were part of the rescue, it was considered as one of our finest hours."

1.3.10 The Other Apollo Landing Missions

The other Apollo landing missions went well, except there was a significant problem during Apollo 12. An hour or so after the astronauts began their activities on the Moon's surface, Conrad accidentally pointed the video camera directly at the sun, and the camera didn't work for the remainder of the mission.

Apollo 14 through Apollo 17 were highly successful missions, and David was involved in planning and supporting each of them. Apollo 15 LM pilot, Jim Irwin, later became a special friend of David. He is the astronaut who experienced some heart abnormalities while on the Moon. He later underwent coronary bypass surgery about a month before David had the same surgery in March of 1977. He and David kept up with each other's health for the remainder of

Jim's life. Jim and Bill Rittenhouse, David's long-time pastor at Nassau Bay Baptist Church (just across from the space center), started an evangelistic organization located in Colorado Springs and called High Flight, which David financially supported for years. Jim passed away in the early-1990's, and David was one of the speakers at his memorial service at Nassau Bay Baptist.

1.3.11 Move to and through NASA Management

Soon after Apollo 17, David was offered a management position on the Division Chief's staff of the Mission Planning and Analysis Division (MPAD). His duties included support for the management of division resources and technical contracts. He served at that position for a couple of years and then received a promotion to the Center's top level, the directorate level. He served on the staff of the Director of the Data System and Analysis Directorate and primarily represented his old division, MPAD. About two years later, he underwent his first coronary bypass surgery, and his doctors recommended that he get out of the high-stress directorate-level job. A few months later, David transferred back to MPAD to a non-management position. However, a few years later, after he was confident that his health was stable, he applied for an assistant division chief position in the Flight Design and Dynamics Division. He was selected for the position over a large number of outstanding applicants, and he remained at that position until he retired from NASA civil service at the end of 1989. For five more years he worked for NASA contractor, Barrios Technology.

1.3.12 NASA Technical Note and AIAA Paper

Shortly after transitioning to his first management job, David co-authored (with co-rendezvous specialist, Bob Becker) a NASA Technical Note and (with co-rendezvous specialist, Ken Young) an American Institute of Aeronautics and Astronautics (AIAA) Paper, each detailing the lunar rendezvous plans and techniques. A NASA Technical Note is one of NASA's top technical documentation levels, and to have a writing published by the AIAA was an honor. David authored many technical documents at various levels during his career (probably at least 100), but the Technical Note and AIAA Paper topped the list.

1.3.13 Must Be a Cowboy, and Other Soviet Stories

Although David had already moved to management, he was asked to support the rendezvous planning for the Apollo Soyuz Test Project (ASTP). ASTP was the Earth-orbit rendezvous mission flown with the Soviets in 1975. The Soviets first put their Soyuz spacecraft into orbit, and then NASA launched the Apollo CSM (from what should have been Apollo 18) and performed a rendezvous with the Soyuz. Apollo 18 had been canceled by Congress to save money—the money saved by not flying Apollo 18 probably funded the nations welfare program for one day, maybe two. Great decision, huh?

During the planning for ASTP, the Soviet engineers and cosmonauts would come to the USA for 2-3 weeks at a time. At the end of each planning visit, they would throw a party at the motel where they stayed and invite the American engineers and astronauts involved in the ASTP planning. At one of these parties, David was pulled aside by one of the Soviet managers along with an interpreter. Through the interpreter, the Soviet said the following to David: "The first time you came into the meeting room, I said to myself, 'This guy can't be a space engineer—he's so big and rugged-looking, he's got to be a cowboy.'"

David and Sandy invited 5-6 of the Soviets (plus an interpreter) along with several of the American engineers to their home for dinner during one of the Soviet planning trips. The Soviets brought several souvenirs, and David still has some of them. One of the Soviet engineers, Olec, was a natural musician, and after dinner he began to play on their organ. At about 11 p. m., the others started telling Olec that it was time to go, but he would say, "Not yet." Finally, at midnight they took him by the arms and legs and carried him out the door.

Most of the Soviets initially couldn't believe that the American engineers really owned their own houses. They thought it was a front set up by our government. Although they were heroes in the Soviet Union, most of them lived in cheap apartments. After coming to the USA two or three times, most of them seemed to be convinced that the American standard of living was for real.

During another of their visits, one of the NASA managers gave a party at his home, and some of the Americans transported the Soviets to and from the party. David and Sandy ended up with only one Soviet in the car with them, and he could speak only a little English. Of course, none of the Americans could speak Russian or any of the other Soviet languages. During the drive to the party, David decided to try to make a little conversation. Speaking very slowly, he asked the Soviet if he was married. The Soviet replied, "Yes, nine years." Then David asked if he had any children. The Soviet replied, "Yes, one son, nine years old."

David glanced at Sandy in the back seat through the rear-view mirror. She was trying to keep from laughing. After about a minute of silence, the Soviet added, "Married ten years."

1.3.14 What Goes Around Comes Around

During his junior year at Baylor, David took a physics course under a young professor, Jerry Fuller, PhD. With only the final exam remaining, David had a grade average of 90. If he could make 90 or above on the final exam, he would get an A in the course. The final exam had nine problems, and was tough. After the exam, several of the students went to the Union Building to have a coke and discuss the exam. When one of the guys mentioned problem #10, several of the other guys, including David, said, "What are you talking about—problem #10?" The guy explained that there was a problem #10 on the back of the exam sheet, and he just happened to notice it when he dropped his exam sheet on the floor. Dr. Fuller did not mention the problem #10 when he handed out the exam, and there was nothing on the front of the exam sheet to indicate that there was an additional problem on the back. Several of the guys, including David, rushed back to the science building to confront Dr. Fuller. He said that he thought he had mentioned the problem #10, but maybe he didn't. Then he promised that he would give a make-up problem to anyone whose final grade might be affected. A few days later he posted final grades, and David had a B. He had made 80 on the final exam, and he again confronted Fuller, but Fuller said it was too late to change the grade. He told David that in the long run, the B would not make any difference in his life. He turned out to be right, but David was very unhappy at the time.

About 11 years later, David was at choir rehearsal at Nassau Bay Baptist Church when Dr. Fuller came walking up. Apparently someone had invited him to the rehearsal. He sat down in a vacant chair a couple of chairs from David and then leaned forward and said to David, "Don't I know you?" David replied, "Yes, I took a physics course under you at Baylor. What are you doing here?" Fuller replied, "I've moved here and started to work for TRW managing the mission planning contract. What about you?" David replied, "I work for NASA and am the NASA manager for the TRW mission planning contract." Fuller got this sickly look on his face and leaned back for a few seconds. Then he leaned forward again and said, "I assume that I'll not get any breaks from you." David simply replied, "Good assumption." Six months later, after a couple of grading periods,

Fuller tried to get transferred off of the contract. About a year later, he quit TRW and started selling mutual funds. What goes around comes around?

1.3.15 Space Shuttle

David was involved in the definition and design of the Space Shuttle. He was one of the mission planning people selected to define what the Shuttle should be able to do, especially relative to maneuvering capability, fuel requirements, etc. Some of the NASA management suggested that the Shuttle would eventually be like a "bus" that would launch every Friday. David assured them that such would probably never happen because of funding limits, safety requirements, and the demand to use essentially 100% of its payload capability every time it launched. David's position proved to be correct. As the Assistant Division Chief of Flight Design and Dynamics, among other duties, David later led in the development of basic plans for updating the flight planning systems to support the Space Shuttle flights.

Although there have been two Shuttle disasters, the Shuttle has had about a 97% success rate. Considering that there are thousands of things that can go wrong (or that have to go right) on each flight, that's a phenomenal success rate.

1.3.16 Shuttle Challenger Disaster

David was in his office, not the Control Center, when the Challenger disaster occurred. Someone screamed from the hallway that the Challenger had exploded. At first, David hoped it was just someone acting silly, but he rushed to a TV to confirm the horrible news. The explosion resulted because a small area of one of the o-rings did not seal correctly, and fuel began to leak during launch. A week or so later, a memorial service was held on the campus of the Johnson Space Center. Present Reagan and several other dignitaries spoke. At the end, the jets flew over and one separated away. David and many others could no longer hold back the tears. It was as if part of their lives had gone down the drain.

1.3.17 Shuttle Columbia Disaster

David and Virginia had been back from their honeymoon just a few days and were having morning coffee at Virginia's Pine Tree house when they heard a big boom. They quickly turned on the TV. As soon as David saw the video of the vapor trails, he said to Virginia, "Oh, no, there's no chance that the crew has survived." About a week later, he was interviewed by Channel 7 TV of Tyler-Longview, and a video of part of the interview was shown on several of their news shows during the next few days. He also was asked to write an article that was published by the White Oak Independent and is presented below. As terrible as the Columbia disaster was for David, at least he did not know the astronauts personally. He had known several of the Challenger astronauts personally, which made that disaster even worse for him.

Local NASA Retiree Discusses Shuttle Tragedy

David Alexander, White Oak High School Class of 1958, was an aerospace engineer and manager at the NASA Johnson Space Center in Houston for 32 years from 1963 to 1995. Early in his career he helped develop plans and techniques for spacecraft rendezvous around both the Earth and the Moon. One of the rendezvous algorithms (software routines) he developed is reportedly still being used by some of our military missiles. He helped train the Apollo astronauts to use the rendezvous plans and techniques, and he supported from the Mission Control Center during the actual missions. He was thereby vitally involved in putting men on the Moon and returning them safely to Earth. During Apollo 13 he helped design the emergency trans-Earth burn that allowed the spacecraft to re-enter the Earth's atmosphere safely. He later was involved in designing the Space Shuttle and its missions. Throughout his career he received awards for both technical and managerial contributions to the space program. In 1993 he was honored as Outstanding Citizen in the Johnson Space Center community. He retired in 1995 and moved back to the Longview area.

Following the Shuttle Orbiter Columbia tragedy Saturday morning, February 1, the Independent called and asked David if he would write an article sharing his thoughts and feelings concerning the tragedy. After some hesitation, he agreed to do so, and the following is what he composed.

Like most patriotic Americans, I am deeply saddened by the Columbia tragedy. First and foremost, I am saddened because of the loss of seven brilliant, brave, and beloved individuals whose families and close friends are devastated but must continue with a tremendous void in their lives. I am also saddened and concerned because I am part of a larger family of past and present members of our nation's space team. At best this tragedy will likely have a negative effect on our space program for at least a year, and maybe several years.

My new wife, Virginia, and I were having coffee in our den when we heard what sounded like a huge explosion shortly after 8 a.m. A few minutes later, the special reports began appearing on TV. As soon as I saw the first videos, I knew the worst had happened. My stomach began to churn and my chest began to ache. Seventeen years ago, when the Challenger exploded during launch, suddenly seemed like yesterday. That same horrible feeling almost paralyzed me. Perhaps the Challenger tragedy was a little worse for me because I was directly part of it. But this tragedy was almost as horrible to me. We space people are a close-knit gang, somewhat like the sports teams I was part of at White Oak and Baylor. We hurt together and we also celebrate together, as was the case three weeks ago when several of my former NASA co-workers drove from Houston to Longview just to attend my wedding.

I will always remember that first Shuttle mission after the Challenger tragedy. A dozen or so of us managers were watching the TV in Gene Kranz's office. Starting about a minute before launch, none of us said a word. Fifteen minutes later when the Shuttle inserted safely into orbit, still none of us could speak. I realized that tears were running down my face, and I started for the door, but I had to stand in line to get out of the room amid a bunch of speechless guys who could only nod their heads and smile through tears.

I did not know the Columbia crew personally, as I did the Challenger crew, but they will also always be my teammates, as will be the crew of Apollo 1 (who died in the Command Module fire on the ground), and as will be the crew of Apollo 13 (who miraculously made it back safely though the odds were heavily stacked against them). Speaking of Apollo 13, I plan to attend a talk by Apollo 13 astronaut Fred Haise on Wednesday, February 4, at Tyler Junior College. I haven't seen Fred for 25 years, and I need to remind him that he owes me.

I believe that during tragic times it helps to remember the good, successful times. Including Projects Mercury, Gemini, Apollo, Skylab, Apollo-Soyuz, and Shuttle, our space program has flown about 147 manned missions. All except three have been successes, and one of the three "failures" (Apollo 13) resulted in, as Gene Kranz suggested, "One of our finest hours." When I remember that thousands of things must go right (or not go wrong) on each of our space flights, I am grateful that our record is as successful as it is. Space flight is not and will never be routine. Unfortunately, many people take it for granted until a tragedy awakens them.

And by the way, the astronauts and scientists who go into space absolutely know the odds of something going wrong and the odds of a fatal tragedy occurring.

Let me attempt to address a few questions and concerns that some of you readers may have. Keep in mind that I'm writing this on Sunday, 1½ days after the tragedy. By the time this article appears in the Independent on Thursday, quite a bit more may be known about what caused the tragedy. But I will make some educated guesses based on my experience with NASA.

First, what may have caused the tragedy? My guess is that the object that broke loose (possibly a large piece of ice or insulation) and struck the wing of the Orbiter during launch may have damaged either the top of the wing or the heat shield on the bottom of the wing. If it damaged the top of the wing, the wing may have malfunctioned when the Orbiter began trying to maneuver (change attitude) during re-entry to keep the heat shield properly aligned, thereby exposing unprotected surfaces of the Orbiter to the tremendous heat. If a section of the heat shield itself (on the bottom of the wing) was damaged during launch, a deterioration of the surrounding heat shield could have occurred, resulting in a sudden meltdown and breakup of the wing or a deterioration of equipment inside the wing. I was on my honeymoon in Hawaii and did not see the launch, and I do not know what was done to try to determine if damage had occurred. But I'm sure that detailed analyses were done.

It may take six months to a year, but I believe the answers will come as to what went wrong. Let's just hope that the impact on our space program will not be permanent or cause major cutbacks. Our space program helped us gain our world leadership status. Our successful Apollo program was a major factor in our winning the Cold War. There are other significant benefits that I will discuss below.

Did the crew know what was happening and did they suffer long? My guess is that within a minute or so (maybe less) of realizing things were hopeless, they became unconscious because of the heat or because of the gravity forces. That is considerably less time than people in tragic airplane crashes usually suffer or agonize.

Was terrorism possibly involved? I would be very surprised if it was. Security for NASA flights is about as tight as it gets.

How will this tragedy affect the International Space Station Program? With my not being a part of the planning anymore, any specific prediction by me would really be a wild guess. We have other Orbiters and the Russians have the Mir, which can transport crews and supplies to and from the Station. But there will definitely be some impact from losing the Columbia.

When a tragedy like this occurs, many people wonder if our space program is worth the costs in money and in lives (a total of 17 deaths have occurred in our manned programs). I won't attempt to answer the "cost in lives" part of the question, but I will briefly address the "money" part. Let me assure you that all of our lives are considerably better, more enjoyable, healthier, and safer because of our space program. Without our space program and its technology spinoffs, we would not have our modern, worldwide TV, phone, and computer communications. Many of our modern medical monitoring, testing, and treatment techniques would probably not exist, and our automobiles and airplanes would not be as safe or as comfortable. There are hundreds of other spinoffs benefit examples. Independent appraisers say that for every dollar that has gone into our space program from day one, twenty dollars worth of technology spinoffs have come back to us to benefit and improve our lives. How many other investments have yielded a 20 to 1 return? And most American families pay (via taxes) less per month to support our space program than the cost of a meal.

By now you are probably not believing that I was hesitant to write this article. I've had to put away my grief and curb my emotion, but I'm glad I wrote it, and I hope it will have some meaning to some of you readers. One reason I agreed to write the article for the Independent is that I still believe that I owe the White Oak community for its contributions to my life. A lot of good things have happened to me, and the road I've traveled began right here in Roughneck country.

If you believe in prayer, please pray for the families of the Columbia crew, for our space program and its leaders, and for our local, national, and world leaders.

May God bless each of you, may God bless White Oak, and may God bless America.

1.3.18 Barrios Technology Employment

David retired early from NASA civil service in order to make sure he would receive the best early-out plan. A year or so later, his early-out plan was no longer available. Several of his long-time co-workers had already retired from NASA and gone to work for one of the NASA contractors—what was referred to as double-dipping (receiving their NASA pensions while working for one of the NASA contractors). David wished to do such and interviewed with several contractors. The president of Barrios Technology, Sandy Johnson, happened to be a lady who had begun her space career right out of college on a contract for which David was the NASA manager. David had encouraged her and helped her get a good start, and they had become friends. She told David to get the best offer he could and she would match it. So David started to work for Barrios and "Boss Sandy," as he called her, in early-1990.

During his five years with Barrios, he was involved mainly with early planning for the International Space Station, specifically on-board crew activity planning. He led in the development of plans to computerize the planning and share the information between organizations and even NASA centers. His work was a forerunner for an internet-type database and data sharing. He met with strong resistance from some of the old heads who were afraid such a plan would allow data to get into the wrong hands or could not be properly maintained and kept current. As it turned out in later years (after David's total retirement), a system to handle most of the Space Station data became a reality.

1.3.19 Total Retirement

David decided to totally retire after he underwent coronary bypass surgery for the second time in June of 1994. He suffered severe complications and spent a total of 46 days in hospitals and missed about 2½ months of work. He retired from Barrios in early-January of 1995 and he and Sandy, who retired from teaching in December of 1994, moved to Longview (Spring Hill) at 219 Goodnight Trail. They lived there only about two years before Sandy's breast cancer recurrence. However, about half of the time during the 3½ years she fought the cancer, she was able to travel, participate in church and community affairs, and pretty much enjoy life.

1.3.20 Space Awards

Throughout his career, David received about seven top NASA awards (Superior Performance, Sustained Superior Performance, etc.) for his technical and managerial contributions to the space program, and he received many other individual and group performance awards. However, perhaps the award that he most cherished was one he received from Barrios Technology about a year before his retirement and which honored him as Outstanding Citizen in the Johnson Space Center Community in 1993. He received this award primarily because of his ministry in Gospel music and his participation as a coach and advisor for youth sports in the area.

1.3.21 Benefits to the General Public from NASA Technology Spinoffs

David seldom gives a speech or talks about his NASA career without mentioning the value of the space program and including some facts about the benefits derived from its technology spinoffs. People are told about the millions of dollars required to fly a space mission or flight, and most people wonder if the NASA space program was and is really worth the cost to the tax payers. The average family pays about $50-$60 per year (or $4-$5 per month) in taxes to support our nation's space program. As a comparison, the average family pays about $5,000-$6,000 per year to support the social programs of our nation. That is, for every $1 paid to support the space program, approximately $100 goes to support the social programs (Welfare, Medicade, certain education programs, etc.). This is not a knock on the social programs, but only a comparison. If the space program were totally canceled and all its funds were given to the social programs, such funds would keep the social programs going for about three days of each year. The NASA budget is approximately one-third of 1% of our total national budget, although many people probably think it's a much larger percentage of our budget.

Independent appraisers estimate that for every dollar ever put into the space program, $20 have come back through technology spinoffs to benefit the general public. Seldom has there been a return on an investment to match that. What are some of the benefits?

1. NASA satellites and commercial satellites put in space by NASA make possible our worldwide telephone, TV, and computer communications.

2. The explosion in computer technology itself was brought about to a large extent by NASA's demand for faster and smaller computers. The computer capability that once required a large room of computer hardware can now be held in one's lap. What once took days to accomplish can now be done in minutes.

3. Modern medical monitoring and testing techniques are the results to some extent of techniques developed to monitor and test the astronauts.

4. Safer and more comfortable automobiles and airplanes are the results of inventions and techniques developed for the space vehicles.

There are hundreds of examples of other benefits. Several books have been published describing them. Plus, there are some things that can not be discussed here that should make every American feel very good about our space program. Hopefully it will suffice here simply to say that all of our lives are better, safer, and more enjoyable because of our space program.

1.3.22 Life Other than on the Earth?

David is often asked if he believes there is or ever has been life other than on the Earth. His answer is that there remain quite a few unexplained occurrences and situations involving both space travel and otherwise. The short answer is that he believes that life elsewhere is not an impossibility. If the Universe were represented by the size of the state of Texas and the Earth were placed thereon, it would be about the size of a pinhead. He has no theological problem with the possibility of life elsewhere in the Universe and knows of nothing in the Bible that says there couldn't be.

1.3.23 Future in Space

David believes that our future in space can be whatever we will allow it to be and whatever we are willing to fund. During the next 10-15 years, hopefully we will follow through with our commitment to go back to the Moon and then put humans on Mars. The more people realize and understand the overall benefits of our space program to the general public and how it pushes technology (see Section 1.3.21), the more they should be willing to support it.

1.3.24 Space-Sports-Music Room (SSMR)

David's SSMR in his and Virginia's home is filled with awards, pictures, and memoirs reflecting these three major involvements in David's life. Included are autographed space program pictures of astronauts (such as the first crew to land on the Moon, and special friend, Apollo 15 's Jim Irwin) and fellow space scientist-engineers (such as legendary leaders Gene Kranz and Chris Kraft). From David's sports career are pictures of teammates, coaches, and championship teams that David was part of. From his music involvement are CD's and cassettes of the recording projects that his quartets have published. Also included are memoirs of some of the achievements of his children, of which he is most proud. If he ever gets a little down, he goes to the SSMR, looks around, and counts his blessings.

1.4 Major Honor, Awards, Achievements, and Activities (Other than through Sports Participation)

1.4.1 High School

David's other high school honors, awards, and achievements included Best All-Round and Scholastic on the Senior Class Hall of Fame; Class Salutatorian; Most Outstanding Student in each math, science, and history; National Honor Society four years; Student Body President; Class President three years; Outstanding Citizenship Awards; and White Oak's Representative to Lone Star Boys' State. He played one of the leading roles in the senior play and sang in several quartets and other singing groups.

1.4.2 College

David's other college honors, awards, and achievements included Distinguished Dean's List and Alpha Chi (3.5/4.0 or better grade-point average); Runner-up for Outstanding Freshman Athlete (combination of athletic and academic achievements); Nominee for Who's Who in American Universities; and Athletes Representative to the Student Council and to the Honor Council. He was also treasurer of his fraternity, Alpha Phi Omega, later converted to the national fraternity, Sigma Alpha Epsilon, and was also selected to escort the 1962 fraternity sweetheart, Linda Moore, originally a Gladewater girl who has remained a friend of David.

1.4.3 As Baylor Alumnus

1.4.3.1 Delivery of Dedication Speech for Coach Patterson Honorary Bust

In April of 2005, honorary busts were dedicated to Baylor's two great track coaches, Jack Patterson (Coach Pat), David's coach, and Clyde Hart, who took the reigns from Coach Pat in 1964 and was head coach for 42 years. Clyde coached three Olympic championship athletes and several more NCAA championship athletes. One of his Olympic champions, Michael Johnson, delivered the dedication speech for Clyde's bust. David was surprised to be chosen to deliver the dedication speech for Coach Pat's bust. Coach Pat had often expressed his pride in David's NASA career and his pleasure in David's contributions as a Baylor trackman, especially after finding out about David's abnormal heart years later.

David was extremely honored not only to be chosen to deliver the dedication speech but also to be on the program with Michael and Clyde. At the end of his speech, David again read a poem he had originally written for Coach Pat several years earlier intended for a special track reunion. Coach Pat died a few months before that reunion, and David read the poem at Coach Pat's memorial service. The poem was later signed by many of Coach Pat's guys and presented to Mrs. Patterson. This same poem was later converted (names changed) to apply for four of David's high school coaches, Coaches Miles, Mullins, Hanicak, and Marshall. Large framed copies, signed by many of the athletes who played for these coaches, were presented to the coaches at White Oak Homecoming in 1997. The poem, as originally written for Coach Pat, is presented below.

To Coach Pat
(For Dedication of Honorary Bust, April 23, 2005)

by David Alexander, Trackman 1959-1962 and Admirer

We've gathered here to reminisce about the good old days
And to thank you, Coach, for all you did in helping to mold our ways;
Our thoughts go back to special times when we were strong and fast,
When you taught us how to be our best and to build on what would last;
We won a lot and had great fun, and we knew by the look in your eyes
That you cherished the joy of our success—we were proud to be your guys;
From winning techniques and fun-filled trips to the times our hearts overflowed,
You were there to share and be our friend—you cared and it clearly showed;
The championships are the icing on the cake of our success,
And without dear Lois' solid support, those times would have meant much less;
We're still your guys and we'll always be, no matter what we face,
For part of you is still with us in life's continuing race;
The years have come and the years have gone and so very much has been,
But we'll always love and honor you, Coach, for helping to make us men.

1.4.3.2 Baylor Letterwinners' Wall of Honor

As a former Baylor letterman, David was selected for this Wall of Honor in 2005 because of extraordinary recognition and honor brought to Baylor through his NASA career and other lifetime achievements. He was the only inductee in 2005 and only the eighth inductee to the Wall of Honor since its inception in 2001. Previous well-known inductees were Hayden Fry, college football coach, and Clyde Hart, Olympic and long-time Baylor track coach. David considered his selection to the Wall of Honor as one of the greatest honors of his life. His special guests at the induction banquet were Virginia, Milli & David Jacks, Greg & Cathy Alexander, Julie & David Anderson and Chase, Lois Patterson (Coach Pat's wife), Tommy Minter & (mom) Louise Erwin, David & Alexis Bennett, Sid & Frankie Alexander, and Bill & Pat McCleary. Below is the wording on his Wall of Honor Plaque displayed in the Baylor Letterwinners' "B" Association Facility. The plaque also contains a picture of David as a Baylor trackman and one when in his mid-60's.

Wording on Wall of Honor Plaque

David Alexander grew up in the oil fields of Northeast Texas. His entire public school career was in the White Oak School District. In high school, he was an exceptional athlete starring on state championship teams in each football, basketball, and track. He was All-State two years in both football and basketball and was All-East Texas in baseball. He still holds White Oak records in all four of these sports. Not only an athlete, he was Class Salutatorian and Student Body President.

At Baylor University, he led his freshman football team in receiving and also lettered in freshman track. Primarily because of health problems (later diagnosed as an abnormal heart), he gave up football early in his sophomore year and concentrated on his track skills where he was a sprinter and a member of the 440, 880, and mile relay teams. He earned three varsity track letters and was a part of SWC track championship teams in 1960 and 1962. As an Honor Student, David was on the Distinguished Dean's List and graduated in 1962 with a B.S. in math-physics.

David began his 32-year career with NASA in 1963. As a mission planner and manager, he was vitally involved in putting men on the Moon, getting the Apollo 13 astronauts back alive, designing the Space Shuttle and its flights, and developing early plans for the Space Station. His technical expertise was orbital rendezvous (bringing two vehicles together in space), particularly around the Moon. He worked directly with the Apollo astronauts and was part of the team that controlled the missions from the Mission Control Center in Houston. He developed a rendezvous algorithm that is reportedly still used in some of our military missiles.

He earned several top NASA awards for technical and managerial contributions and was also honored as Outstanding Citizen in the Johnson Space Center Community.

Beginning at age 12, David has regularly used his baritone voice in church choirs and Gospel quartets. He has composed and published 14 Gospel songs.

David's first wife, Sandy, was also a White Oak and Baylor University graduate. She taught school for 27 years before she died from cancer in 2000. David married his second wife, Virginia, in 2003, and they live in White Oak. His daughter, Milli Jacks, is a graduate of Baylor and Baylor Law School, and his son, Greg, is a NASA computer guru.

1.4.4 NASA

During his 32-year career with the space program, David received several top NASA awards and many other individual and group awards for both technical and managerial contributions, but the award that he cherished as much as any was one he received in 1993, a year or so prior to his retirement when he was selected as the recipient of Barrios Technology Emy Award, honoring him as Outstanding Citizen in the Johnson Space Center Community.

1.5 MUSIC INVOLVEMENT

David began taking piano lessons at age 7. His adopted sister, Carolyn, was a very talented pianist, and because their parents chose for her to take piano lessons, they decided that David should also take piano lessons. Although he did not possess the natural talent to play the piano and other instruments well, he did learn enough about music to later enjoy singing, arranging, and composing. To date he has composed about 14 songs (lyrics and voice parts), has composed the voice parts (music) for several other songs for which the lyrics have been written by others, and has arranged many other songs for the quartets in which he has sung. His choir arrangements for several of his original songs have also been preformed by the adult choirs at Mobberly Baptist Church and at Nassau Bay Baptist

Church. David took piano lessons for about five years but quit taking piano at age 12 due to conflicts with sports involvements.

David never took a voice lesson. Although he does not have a high-quality voice, he hears all harmony parts and prefers to sing harmony. His natural singing range is baritone, which he has typically sung in quartets and other ensembles. He began singing tenor in the adult choir at Spring Hill Baptist Church at age 11 and usually sat beside "Uncle" Earl Meadows, who often took David, Carolyn, and other young people to Sunday afternoon singings all around East Texas. David also sang tenor in the first quartet in which he sang (at age 12). It was a mixed quartet in which sister Carolyn sang alto, and a couple of older teenagers, Janice Martin and Gene Dickson, sang soprano and bass. Through the years, starting in high school, David has sung in a couple of other mixed quartets and about five male quartets. His current quartet, Four-Ever His (formerly called Thee Mobb Quad), started in 1996. David and Mark Johnson, the second tenor, were in the original quartet. The original first tenor, Jon Harvey, and the original bass, David Sledge, were replaced by Rick Anderson in 1999 and Tommy Herndon in 2001, respectively. Four-Ever His averages 15-20 engagements per year and has published two projects (recordings). The first recording included two of David's newer original songs. Twelve of David's fourteen original songs have thus far been published.

David sang with The Master's Vessels quartet during his last 12½ years in the Houston area (while working at NASA). The same four guys sang together for about nine years before bass David Leake suddenly died from a stroke. He was replaced by Bill Durham during the last four years. Ron Sanford, the first tenor, and Dallas Anderson, the second tenor, and David ministered together for the full 12½ years until David retired and moved back to the Longview area. The Master's Vessels averaged 40-45 engagements per year and sang 2-3 times per year at Lakewood Church, one of the largest churches in the nation. They published seven projects, which included ten of David's original songs.

David has sung with the Men of Praise, the 24-voice men's ensemble at Mobberly Baptist Church, since 2001. He and Virginia sing in Mobberly's 150-voice adult choir, The PraiSingers, and also in the senior choir, People of Praise Singers, when special performances are involved.

The dedications for David's 14 original songs are included below. He recently found in an old storage box a copy of the very first song he composed in 1953 at about age 13. The words for each of his original songs are included in Section 7.

Individual Song Dedications of David Alexander's Original Songs

(In Chronological Order of Composition, with Date of Composition Indicated)

I Am on My Way to the Glorious Day (1953): All of David's sports coaches, particularly Moon Mullins, Cotton Miles, and Jack Patterson (dedication made in 2007 after song found in storage box 54 years after written).

Sometimes I'd Like to Go Back (October 1984): Cat, David's sister, and the Tom Jankowskis, friends of the best kind.

Thank You, Jesus, for Calvary (April 1985): George & Olga Alexander, David's loving parents, and Bob Culpepper, a friend indeed.

My Crown at His Feet (April 1986): Dr. Hal & Pat Boone, inspirational friends and wonderful Christian examples, and The Paul Gilmores, great, fun friends.

Let My Life Reflect Your Love (January 1987): Sandy, David's beautiful first wife, whose life truly reflected God's love.

It's Time We Pulled Together (June 1987): All of The Master's Vessels, wives, and families, and the Paul LeBlancs, great "Cajun" and Catholic friends.

I'm Excited (July 1987): Milli and Greg, David's wonderful children, and all youth in general.

Precious Lord, in My Heart I Love You (August 1987): Frankie "Sunshine" Alexander, David's aunt and long-distance prayer partner, and Sid & Frankie Alexander, David's old "roomie" and special friends.

Through Faith by Grace (May 1988): Dr. Bill & Nell Rittenhouse, long-time pastor and friends, and John & Helen Ginga, special prayer partners (especially concerning this song).

He's in Control (November 1990): The Tommy Minters, David's cousin and "Best Man" and his family, and the Canions, other great relatives.

When He Gave His All for Me (March 1991): H. E. & Aline Bingham, David's great parents-in-law, and Dutch & Betty Schroeder, great "Bear" friends.

Eternal Day (June 1994): Thee Mobb Quad/Four-Ever His and families, and Bill & Pat McCleary, dear, helpful friends.

Men of Old (September 1996): Dr. Laney & Emily Johnson, and Dale & Shirley Perkins and all their families.

Without Faith We Cannot Please Our Father Up Above (August 2001): Virginia, David's wonderful second wife, and her families.

1.6 OTHER INTERESTS AND INVOLVEMENTS

David's interests and involvements other than space, sports, and music have been primarily in other church activities and service, contributions (financial and otherwise) to his alma maters (White Oak Schools and Baylor University), assistance in youth sports, and limited involvement in political activities.

In addition to music involvement in church, he has served as a deacon and a Bible study teacher. He was ordained as a deacon in the Nassau Bay Baptist Church in 1976 at age 36. He has contributed significantly to various scholarship and educational funds at White Oak and Baylor. He was the only Platinum Level ($25,000) founding contributor to White Oak's Education Foundation, founded in 2001, and a $1,000+ scholarship is awarded to an outstanding student-athlete graduate each year with the interest earned on the funds endowed from his contribution. He has later donated several thousand dollars more to the White Oak Education Foundation. He has also given substantial amounts to Baylor for such projects as the "B" Association (Letterwinners') facility extension, improvements to the Baylor's Hart-Patterson Track & Field Complex and honorary busts for these two legendary coaches, building of the Dutch Schroeder Baseball-Softball Stadiums Walkway, basketball practice facility, and recruiting facility. He is a lifetime member of the "B" Association (thanks to Dutch Schroeder) and a member of the "B" Association's 100 Club, to which he donates $1,000 per year. He periodically sends letters of congratulations and encouragement to students, athletes, coaches, and teachers. He has helped coach summer youth baseball as a pitching and hitting coach and has regularly financially supported youth sports.

He was a leader of the team in League City that implemented a Proposition 13-type effort to slow the rapid rise in city taxes in the late-1970's, and he has financially contributed significantly through the years to political candidates and efforts sharing his basic political views and agendas.

1.7 FONDEST MOMENTS AND MEMORIES (OTHER THAN SPORTS)

If the title of this section were "*Very Fond* Moments and Memories" instead of "*Fondest* Moments and Memories," this section would be several pages long. Among David's *fondest* moments and memories have been his weddings to Sandy and Virginia (and honeymoons), the births and weddings of his children, special times with his grandchildren, Milli's receiving Clear Creek High School's Weber Award (for being selected the outstanding all-round student in her class) and being selected as one of the ten Outstanding Senior Women in her Baylor class, Greg's receiving Student of the Year and top NASA awards and being recognized as one of the top computer gurus in the NASA arena, David's being part of the Moon landings and other special NASA successes, David's being selected as Outstanding Citizen in the Johnson Space Center Community, the Alexander family singing performances when Milli and Greg were young and at Mobberly Baptist Church on Christmas Eve of 2000, his 40th birthday party, his 60th birthday party and book of letters prepared by Milli, and his being inducted to the Baylor Letterwinners' Wall of Honor with family and some of dearest friends present.

1.8 HARDEST AND SADDEST TIMES

Among the hardest and saddest times in David's life have been Sandy's illnesses with cancer and her death, granddaughter Ali's sudden accidental death, David's dad's sudden death, David's own heart problems and surgeries (especially the second surgery), and the three space program tragedies. Although he loved his mother very much, her death at age 89 was a blessing because her health had deteriorated terribly and she was definitely ready to leave this world.

1.9 SPECIAL REASONS FOR THANKSGIVING

Among the many blessings for which David is especially thankful are his wonderful parents, his two beautiful wives, his super children and grandchildren, his talented sister, his great relatives and friends, his being part of the White Oak and Baylor heritages, his having the doctors and medicines to keep him alive in spite of his severe heart disease, his being born in the USA, and his being born at the time he was born. Had he been born 15-20 years earlier, he probably would have died before he was forty because of his heart disease. Had he been born 15-20 years later, his heart disease probably would have been detected when he was an early teenager, and he probably would not have been allowed to participate in sports. Had he been born 5-10 years earlier or later, he probably would not have been directly involved in putting men on the Moon. God's timing is always best. The medical doctors for whom David is especially thankful are George Marcom (GP), Neal Watkins (GP), Efrain Garcia (Cardiologist), Denton Cooley (Heart

Surgeon), Neil Marshall (GP), Rodney Henry (Cardiologist), and Lawrence Roe (IM). Interestingly, Watkins, Cooley, Marshall, and Henry all did their pre-med studies at Baylor University.

1.10 THEOLOGICAL BELIEFS

The following are some of David's key theological beliefs and convictions. Each statement or thought should be considered to begin with "David believes that …," and where "he" is used, it is intended to mean "he or she."

There is an Almighty God who has the knowledge and power to totally rule and control the Universe, but He chooses to allow mankind to partly control his own destiny. Relative to individuals, God knows everything that CAN happen, but He chooses to limit Himself such that He does not know and control everything that WILL happen. Some say that God has no limits, but the Bible indicates that He does have limits which He places on Himself. For example, the Bible says that once a person truly confesses his sins and asks God for forgiveness, God can no longer remember those sins because He separates those sins from Him as far as the east is from the west. If God knows and controls everything that WILL happen (total predestination), then humans are nothing more than puppets, and we make no choices and have no will—and life really has no meaning. What is predestined are God's physical, moral, and spiritual laws. If we violate such laws, then the consequences are predestined. Whereas, if we observe and obey such laws, wonderful results are predestined.

Some say that because we do not know the future, then, in a way, we do have a will. But if everything is already fixed and decided, then there really is no human will or choices. Why would God create humans to love and worship Him if they had no choice? How could that possibly please Him?

Jesus Christ is the divine Son of God and came to Earth to become the sacrifice for our sins and to make possible the free gift of Salvation. But for our sins to be forgiven and to share in God's Kingdom forevermore, we must accept that gift and make Jesus Christ our Savior and Lord. God initially elected all humans to share eternity with Him. He did not will that any should perish. But sin came into the world, making it necessary for each human to repent of his sins and accept God's gift of Salvation (that whosoever believes …) in order to inherit everlasting life in the Kingdom of God. If God determined before the foundations of the world who would be and who would not be forever in His Kingdom, then why have churches, why have evangelism, why not just eat, drink, and be merry? If there is an elect, they will be in God's Kingdom regardless of what anyone does or doesn't do, and those not elected have no chance and were doomed from the start. We are all doomed because of sin if we do not accept the gift of Salvation. If everything were decided from the start, that would make God horribly cruel to send His only Son to suffer and die for no reason—because the elect would have already been decided.

God does not have just one plan for each person. He has trillions upon trillions of plans or paths for each person and largely allows that person to choose the paths he will travel. When a person truly chooses Jesus Christ as his Savior and Lord, it's as if God attaches a tether to that person to prevent him from going down a path that totally separates him from God. If the person heads down the wrong paths, eventually God will draw that person back to Him. Prayer and Bible study help us determine God's will (the best paths) for our lives. Without prayer and Bible study and the assistance of the Holy Spirit, we cannot understand the truth about the scriptures and various other aspects of theology. We should not accept something because it's exciting or makes us part of a majority or a minority view. But if one strongly senses that the Holy Spirit is telling him that something is right or true, and such does not contradict the scriptures, he should go with it and not worry about what anyone else believes.

Without faith we cannot please God. If we knew all the answers and could see all God's ways, there would be no need for faith. If we knew why the righteous suffer and the wicked seem to prosper (for a while), and if we knew why terrible tragedies occur, there would be no need for faith. If God had wanted to set it up such that we knew and understood everything, He could have, but He did not. So we must have faith that "all things work for the good of them who love and obey God and answer His call to worship and serve Him." Good will ultimately overcome evil.

Humans have a spirit, and only when God's Spirit, the Holy Spirit, becomes part of a person's spirit can that person truly know God, know true happiness and fulfillment, and know that he is and always will be part of God's Kingdom. When God's Spirit fills a person's spirit, that person will desire to worship and serve God and to use his gifts and talents and resources to bring praise and glory to God. If he gives in the right spirit and for the right reasons, one cannot outgive God, and it is far more blessed to give than to receive, relative to God and mankind.

1.11 PHILOSOPHICAL THOUGHTS AND OPINIONS

Although one cannot control everything in his life and enviror have a lot to do with what he is and becomes. If he applies hims does his best, the odds are good that he will amount to somethin will be happy with what he becomes. Hanging tough someti tempted to give up or take an easier path can result in a big   s future. On the other hand, it is important for one to realize ar   ts and be realistic about his abilities and potential. Two of David's favorite sayings are, "Success is not being THE best, success is being YOUR best," and "You do your best, and He will do the rest."

One's success in life can be partly measured by the happiness and success of his spouse and children. Another measure of success is in the number of close friends one has. Friends, including relatives who are friends, are among one's greatest possessions. The greatest honors are to be loved and respected, and the greatest privileges are to give and serve.

A sense of humor is indeed important in obtaining happiness and success. Laughing not only is helpful to one's physical and mental health, it is also a plus toward building special friendships. People who laugh together usually remain special friends. One must be able to laugh with others and at himself.

There are basically happy people and unhappy people, although a person can probably change from an unhappy person to a happy person with enough effort. Happy people are happy unless something temporarily makes them unhappy. Unhappy people are unhappy unless something temporarily makes them happy. Happy people tend to dwell on the positive and on God's love, mercy, grace, and blessings toward them. Unhappy people tend to dwell on the negative and how they have been mistreated or cheated out of what they deserve. They seldom express thanks or gratitude but instead dwell on what they don't have or on the small percentage of something that they don't like. Counting blessings is a great way to overcome unhappiness. Each new day should be considered a blessing, and we can thank God for each day by using it to try to accomplish something worthwhile, especially something that will bring praise and glory to Him.

1.12 POLITICAL VIEWS AND OPINIONS

The major continual differences between Republicans and Democrats are (a) how much and whom to tax and how to use the taxes, and (b) how much to allow minority demands to rule the majority, such as how much to limit freedom of religion to avoid offending the minority, and such as how much to allow certain things and actions that the majority consider immoral to appease the minority.

Every great civilization (empire) that has failed has essentially followed the same path to failure or mediocrity. They have condoned immoral behavior, both homosexual and heterosexual. Further, the masses have found a way to take control of the government and legislate income to themselves and their friends (or live off of the government) while essentially doing nothing to deserve such compensation.

Neither of the major political parties is all good or all bad. Both have positives and negatives. Both agree that the "rich" should share their wealth with the "poor." The difference lies in where the line should be drawn. In later years, David has aligned himself primarily, but not totally, with the Republican Party because he believes their basic philosophy is best for the current and future generations of our nation; that is, basically capitalism instead of socialism.

1.13 FAVORITE THINGS

Food—Country, like meatloaf, chicken-fried steak, beans/peas and cornbread, grilled steak or shish-kabob, pecan or fruit pie (cherry or banana), Mexican food

Hobbies/Past-times—Sports fan, live or on TV (football, basketball, baseball, or track from high school through pros); music singing or listening (mainly Gospel and Christian classic); travel (cruising, touring, to visit kin or friends)

Sports Teams—NFL (Cowboys, Saints, Colts); NBA (Mavericks, Rockets, Spurs); Major League Baseball (Astros, Rangers); College sports (Baylor, other State of Texas teams, other Big 12 teams)

Pro Athletes—NFL (Payton Manning, Mike Singletary, Don Meredith, Max McGee); NBA (Michael Jordon, Dirk Nowitsky, Ken Duncan, Wilt Chamberlain)

Movies (all-time)—Ben Hur, Elmer Gantry, It's a Wonderful Live, The Greatest Story Ever Told

Movie Stars (all-time)—Burt Lancaster, James Stewart, Charleston Heston, Jack Palance, Jack Lemon, Denzell Washington, Julia Roberts, Meg Ryan, Aubrey Hepburn

Comedians—Bob Hope, Johnathan Winters, Don Rickles, Rodney Dangerfield

Pastors—Bill Rittenhouse (Nassau Bay Baptist Church), John Morgan (Sagemont Church), Laney Johnson (Mobberly Baptist Church)

1.14 Unfavorite Things

Food—Anchovies, coconut, broccoli

Other—When someone sitting behind you at a theater, ballgame, church, etc., continuously bumps the back of your seat; when folks are continually negative about our nation or life in general

2

Immediate Family

2.1 First Wife, Sandra "Sandy" Elaine Bingham Alexander

Most people assume that David and Sandy had one of the best marriages that there could be, and David assures that they are absolutely right. He says that he could count on one hand the disagreements and tense moments between Sandy and him, and even those times were short-lived. He says that almost any guy could have been happy married to Sandy, and that he just happened to have been the fortunate one.

David and Sandy knew of each other most of their lives, as they both grew up in White Oak. Sandy was about 20 months younger and one grade behind David. She graduated in the White Oak Class of 1959. While in high school she was a varsity cheerleader and the Texas State President of the Future Homemakers of America. David often joked that she must have spent most of her time making speeches because it took her years after they were married to become a good cook.

Although they never dated in high school and not until Sandy's junior year at Baylor, Sandy often made it known that David had been her hero since her early teenage years. They dated some "just as friends" during the summer before David's senior year at Baylor, and then he took her to some fraternity functions the next fall. Not realizing that Sandy was falling in love with him, David started dating another young lady named Zelda. He had a date planned with Zelda on a March Sunday evening upon returning with the track team from the Border Olympics in Laredo. When he got back to Waco, a guy from Zelda's hometown came to David's dorm room and informed him that Zelda had the mumps and would not be returning to Waco for 2-3 weeks. As David began considering whom he might ask for a short-notice date, he remembered that a month or so

57

earlier a track teammate had asked him how long it had been since he had seen Sandy. The teammate said she had really shaped up and was gorgeous. David decided to take a look for himself, and he called Sandy, whom he had not seen for several months, and asked her out to the movies. After briefly hesitating, she accepted but asked David to pick her up at a dorm other than the one where she lived. That was the evening David began to fall in love with Sandy. She later told him that she already had a date that evening with the guy she had been dating regularly. When she returned to her dorm after she and David's date, the other guy was still waiting for her. She apologized but told him that she was in love with David. Even mumps can be a good thing. Sandy and David never dated anyone else after that.

Sandy was an average student in high school and then in college until David encouraged her to become a good student. She made the Distinguished Dean's List for all A's her last semester at Baylor. Because of a birth-defect hearing problem, she always tried to sit near the front of the class so she could read the professor's lips. She later further demonstrated her high intellect by becoming an outstanding teacher. A guy on a cruise once told Sandy that children get their "basic smarts" from their mother, and she could hardly wait to return home and enlighten Milli and Greg.

Sandy made the long trip by car with David's parents and sister, Carolyn, and Carolyn's two pre-school sons, Ken and David, to Corona, California, to visit David in August of 1962. David had accepted a job at the Naval Ordnance Lab there in June, and he and Sandy had not seen each other for about two months. During the visit, David gave Sandy an engagement ring, and they set a wedding date for mid-February of 1963, thinking they would be living in California after their wedding.

However, in early January of 1963 David found out that NASA had begun hiring in Texas for the space center in Houston, and he called and got a job with NASA. He began working for NASA in early February, about two weeks prior to their wedding on February 16, 1963. He was given a week of advanced leave so that they could honeymoon in Dallas and get Sandy moved to Houston.

David and Sandy's first home was in the brand-new Royal Wayside Apartments on East Wayside Drive about five miles southeast of downtown Houston. The space center was not completed at that time, and the division for which David worked was housed in some office buildings on the Gulf Freeway (I-45) about a mile from the newly weds' apartment. David could rush home, eat lunch, etc., and be gone from work less than an hour.

Sandy got a job at Houston ISD's Pugh Elementary where she taught during the fall of 1963 and the spring of 1964. David's division moved down to the space center in the summer of 1964, and he and Sandy moved to the Carriage Square Apartments in Dickinson. They lived there for about two years before they moved in June of 1966 into the new home they built at 1907 Rampart Street in League City, where they lived for 28½ years.

Sandy taught in Dickinson for two years before she began her 21-year teaching career with the Clear Creek ISD, including two years before Milli was born and then 19 years after Greg started to school. Sandy's teaching career also included three years at the Nassau Bay Baptist Church Pre-School during Milli and Greg's pre-school years. She taught 27 years altogether, including a total of 24 years in public school systems. She was a greatly loved and highly respected and requested teacher throughout her teaching career. After the dreaded teacher evaluation system began in the mid-1980's, she always received the highest evaluation possible.

Sandy was a wonderful wife and mother, everything David had dreamed possible. She was a calm, easy-going, but charismatic and optimistic person. Everyone who really knew her really loved her. People quickly realized that she was as beautiful on the inside as she was on the outside. For her memorial service, David composed a tribute to her, which was read by one of their special NASA friends, Bob Culpepper. The tribute, as included below, was later published in several local newspapers.

A Tribute to Sandy

(Written by David for Sandy's Memorial Service on October 27, 2000)

Sandra Elaine Bingham Alexander, known to most of us as Sandy, was born August 15, 1941, in Longview, Texas, the younger of two daughters of H. E. "Bill" and Aline Bingham of White Oak. The Bill Binghams were one of White Oak's most respected and involved families for more than 50 years.

Sandy attended White Oak Schools from 1st through 12th grade. She was a varsity cheerleader and a leader in the Future Homemakers of America, serving as statewide president her senior year.

She attended Baylor University where she received a Bachelor of Arts Degree in Elementary Education and made the Distinguished Dean's List (for all A's) her senior year. She and Dave professed their love for each other near the end of her junior year and Dave's senior year at Baylor. Though they both were from White Oak, they were not high school sweethearts. Yet, Sandy often made it known that

Dave had been her hero since her early teenage years. One of the last things she said to Dave was that he was still her hero. Of course, she long ago indeed became Dave's heroine.

They were married on February 16, 1963, two weeks after Dave began his career with NASA. According to Dave, Sandy was a wife more wonderful than he'd ever dreamed possible and was the main reason most people who really knew them considered them to have an ideal marriage.

Sandy was a marvelous mother, greatly loved and honored by her two children, Milli and Greg, who brought much pleasure and pride to her because of their success and Christian lives. Milli is an attorney and the mother of 1-month-old David Lee Jacks, II, who was born six hours before Sandy left this world. Greg is a top computer guru for a NASA contractor and the father of granddaughters Ali, Caitlin, and Megan. Sandy has recently been reunited with Ali, who has been waiting in Heaven for her Gammy for nearly 3½ years.

Sandy was a delightful, fun grandmother, always ready to manifest her love to her grandchildren whether by reading, singing, or playing baby dolls with them.

Sandy was a beloved mother-in-law to son-in-law David Jacks and daughter-in-law Cathy Duke Alexander.

Sandy was a cherished sister to Janis Canion, of whom she was very proud because of Janis' tremendous accomplishments as an educator and citizen in the Longview area.

Sandy was a wonderful cousin to her "look-alike" first cousin, Betty Laura King, who was more like a sister to her.

Sandy was a much loved, devoted daughter, daughter-in-law, niece, sister-in-law, and aunt; and she was a favorite among her many other relatives and special friends. She had a large number of dear loved ones, ranging in age from the 90's down to pre-teens, who regularly visited, called, or wrote to her. They're from early White Oak days, Baylor, Houston/NASA area, post-retirement Longview area, and elsewhere.

Sandy was one of the most respected and requested elementary school teachers in the Clear Creek Independent School District. She taught several children of the astronauts and of top NASA managers, scientists, and engineers, and many others who gave her much credit for later success. But she was best known for her handling and developing of students with serious discipline and emotional problems. Because of her kind and loving approach, many of these problem students became good, successful students.

Sandy was a fine, natural musician, playing the piano for most of the Gospel quartets that Dave sang in through the years. She also led the singing or played piano for children's churches for several years. She was a unique ventriloquist. She loved to shop, travel, read, bake goodies for favorite people, and visit with cherished relatives and friends.

Most of all, Sandy was one of the most beautiful human beings, inside and out, that many of us have ever known. She exhibited incredible faith, love, grace, compassion, tolerance, and optimism. Her mere presence was a blessing. She was an encourager and a giver. One of her final wishes was to donate her physical body to research. She loved people, and she loved and honored her Lord. The world is definitely a better place because she dwelt here for 59+ years.

In September, she was unable to attend a White Oak Homecoming reception, but she sent a letter that included a request that I believe she would also intend for all of us. She wrote, "Keep a smile and a bit of cheer from me within your heart, and should you encounter someone along your way who really needs it, please give some of it to them for me. That would make me so happy."

As far as we know, Sandy wrote only one poem in her lifetime, but it was a beauty. She and David were on a trip to New England with Betty (Sandy's first cousin) and Gene King in the fall of 1995 when Sandy was inspired to write the poem while motoring through New York State. David helped perfect the meter, but the content was from Sandy.

Autumn Inspiration

Leaves of cinnamon, crimson, and wine,
Shades of green and gold intertwined,
Variety of shape and awesome hue,
Giving to all a breathtaking view,

As if with Heavenly paintbrush in hand,
God stroked vivid colors o'er the
    mountainous land;
I gaze in wonder at the marvelous sight,
Assured of His presence, love, and great might.

Lord, put on Your easel the canvas of
    my life

And create a Masterpiece, filled with love,
　　free of strife.

By Sandy Alexander
New England Trip
September 29, 1995

A few months after David fell in love with Sandy, he wrote for her the poem, "To Sandy, My Love," which she always cherished. It has been reformatted for this book and is as follows:

To Sandy, My Love

(June, 1962)

Part I: Concepts of Love

'Tis said that true love can't be fully explained, for its meaning completely no
　　words have contained;
Attraction and prestige, though each plays a part, are really just luxuries that give
　　love a start;
The important things that make love so grand are honor and trust and faith that
　　will stand,
A deep understanding, the will to be true, attempts to make happy in all each
　　can do;
True love plays no games nor prides in deceiving, but joys in giving much more
　　than receiving;
It plans for the future and learns from the past and builds its foundation on
　　things that will last;
And as for the present it yearns to be near that wonderful person who makes
　　life so dear;
Love brings a great feeling deep down in the heart that pleasure nor sadness can
　　cause to depart.

Part II: Thoughts of My Love

As I sit at evening and think of My Love, I lift my head humbly toward
　　Heaven above

And thank God sincerely for sending to me My Wonderful Sandy, the best there
could be!

I pray I'll deserve such a lady so fine and that such an angel will someday
be mine;

I know that her tender, warm, sweet loving ways will fill me with joy throughout
all my days;

For when she comes near me, my heart skips a beat, and then I know surely
she'll make life complete;

Her love is so precious and matchless to me, without it to cherish,
no future I'd see;

But with her beside me, so sound and mature, let come good or bad, all things
we'll endure;

My love grows much stronger with each passing day—believe me, My Sandy,
this love's sure to stay.

Part III: My Prayer of Love

Oh God, in my thankfulness I offer this prayer: "Help us to prove love and
always be fair;

Let our love prosper and always be true, and help us look upward in
all that we do;

Don't let the awful confusions of life plague our young love with
sorrow and strife;

But show us the right ways and help us to be full of deep understanding and
warm sympathy;

And give us that moment when standing so proud we'll take vows of marriage
before You and the crowd;

Then give us the good things that life has in store and help us mold young lives
that You can adore;

And through all the joys and sorrows life brings, cause us to praise You for all
the good things;

And when we come finally to life's last few miles, keep our love strong then and
give our hearts smiles."

Yes, life is worth living since God up above sent me My Sandy and
    taught me to love!

I love you, Angel,
David

On their 12th wedding anniversary (February 16, 1975) David wrote the following sonnet for Sandy.

AN ANNIVERSARY SONNET TO SANDY
(From David, on Our 12th Wedding Anniversary, February 16, 1975)

My Angel Wife, although twelve years have passed,
My love for you has never ceased to grow,
And always I have known that it would last
And e'er fulfill and set my heart aglow.

My Love, to me you've been a constant joy,
A source of inspiration, pride, and cheer
That time and familiar ways could not destroy
But rather bring assurance and endear.

Your love for Mil and Greg, your joyful zest,
Your exciting touch, your tender loving smile,
The care you take to always look your best,
Are among the reasons I've loved you all the while.

I thank our Lord for you each time I pray—
And for making you so beautiful in every way.

For Mother's Day of 1997, David wrote to Sandy the following letter:

Sandy, My Love,
    Even in my most optimistic expectations as a young man, I never dreamed of
having such a beautiful, magnificent wife, friend, and lover as you.
    What a wonderful life and marriage we've had—with more fun, joy, blessings,
and love than we might have expected to have in 200 years.
    Never once have I doubted my love for you, and never once have I doubted
your love for me.

What beautiful kids we've raised—each possessing a blend of our best qualities and genes. And what an ideal mother, mother-in-law, and grandmother you've been and are (and again will be).

Thanks for sharing your love and encouragement so freely with all who need it. You make me so proud. You're my heroine!

Two of my very favorite things are still just "looking at you" and "feeling your touch." Yes, when I'm near you, my heart still skips a beat.

You're more than my dream wife, and more than ever

> I love you,
> David

For Mother's Day of 1999, David wrote to Sandy the following:

Some A, B, C's of Why *I Love My Sandy,* Because she is

A—Angelic, Amazing, Adorable, Admirable, Affectionate, Affable

B—Beautiful, Breathtaking, Bright, Blessed, Believing, Brave, Best

C—Classy, Compassionate, Considerate, Cordial, Colorful, Creative,
    Clever, Calm, Clean, Courteous, Courageous, Consistent

D—Delightful, Desirable, Delicious, Dedicated, Dependable

E—Excellent, Elegant, Enthusiastic, Easy-Going, Encouraging

F—Fabulous, Fun, Friendly, Faithful, Forgiving, First-Class

G—Gorgeous, Glamorous, Graceful, Gracious, Giving, Grateful, Genuine

H—Heavenly, Holy, Happy, Honest, Humble

I—Incredible, Immaculate, Ideal, Irrepressible

J—Joyful, Jubilant, Just

K—Kind, Keen, Kissable

L—Loving, Lovable, Luscious, Literary

M—Marvelous, Magnificent, Merciful, Musical, Meek

N—Nice, Neat, "Novelistic"

O—Outstanding, Optimistic, Outgoing

P—Pretty, Polished, Positive, Peaceful, Pure, Polite

Q—Quality, Queenly

R—Regal, Romantic, Real, Rare, Respectable, Reliable, Renown, Relaxed

S—Spiritual, Sensitive, Submissive, Sensational, Sexy, Sharp, Sweet,
    Stable, Super-Shopper, "Scratchy"

T—Talented, Thoughtful, Trustworthy, Tenderhearted

U—Understanding, Upright, Uplifting, Uncommon

V—Victorious, Virtuous, Vivacious, Versatile
W—Wonderful, Wise, Wholesome, Well-Born, Witty
X—Xerox copy of a Lady and a Doll
Y—Youthful, "Yogurty"
Z—Zealous, Zion-Bound

> Happy Mother's Day (May 9, 1999)
> Love,
> David

For David's 60th birthday in November 1999, Sandy wrote to him a wonderful letter (about ten months before her death), which reads as follows:

Dear Precious David,

You and the Lord have made my life Heaven on Earth. To think that you could have had any woman in the world, and you chose me!! These past 37 years have been filled with such love, joy, excitement, and stability that I can only say, "To God be the Glory!" He has never failed us; rather, He just keeps blessing.

As each day passes, I find myself loving you more. After all these years my heart continues to sing, "He's mine!" Never have I doubted your love and devotion to me. You show it in so many ways.

We've shared so much! How I treasure the memories of travel (especially cruises), family, friends, careers, quartets, etc. Has any other couple had half as much fun in a lifetime as we've had in a day? And then we've had the "lows"—a time of refining and learning to lean on Jesus. I'm so thankful we've walked hand in hand on this journey of life.

You've always been my hero, and I've never failed to be proud of my "he man." I dearly love this capable side of you, but I am equally touched by your tender, gentle compassion for Mom in the sunset of her life. You are the son she always wanted. She's loved and trusted you without reservation. Thank you for honoring me in this way.

I'm grateful that you've been the Christian leader in our home. What a wonderful example you have set for Milli and Greg. (At least they got their brains from me!)

May you always be aware of the love, respect, dignity, and goodness that I have found in you.

Happy birthday to my lover, my best friend, my constant guardian, and my matchless husband on this your 60th year.

As you wrote in June, 1962:
"And when we come finally to life's last few miles
Keep our love strong then, and give our hearts smiles."

Love,
Sandy

2.2 Second Wife, Mary Virginia McGraw Ouzts Alexander and Family

David met Virginia through their Bible study department at Mobberly Baptist Church about four months after Sandy died. Virginia's first husband (of 43 years), Sam, had died, also from cancer, in August of 2000. Virginia knew of David before they actually met because of his quartet singing in the worship services, and David had noticed Virginia but actually didn't know who she was. They were at lunch with a group from church after Bible Study on a Sunday in mid-February of 2001 when a friend asked Virginia if she was planning to attend the Bible Study class party that coming weekend. Virginia replied that she wasn't planning to attend because she didn't yet care to go out at night alone. After about ten seconds of total group silence, David, who was sitting across the table from Virginia, asked her if she would be interested in attending the party if he were to "give her a ride," and then added, "I'll go if you'll go." After another long group silence, a red-faced Virginia replied, "Well, I uh, uh guess so." After lunch, David and Virginia got together and made sure they knew each other's names and phone numbers.

During the next few days, they both had serious thoughts about going through with this "date." Several times during the last few months of her life, after there was no hope of recovery short of a miracle, Sandy had made it clear to David that she did not want him to wait very long after her death to "get back into circulation." She said she did not want him to be alone for long, especially if he could find a special female companion. David did not make any promises to Sandy, but his remembrance of her wishes encouraged him to go through with this first date with Virginia. They were the center of attention at the party, and went to a movie afterward.

They continued to see each other once or twice a week during the next few months by going out to eat, attending church functions, watching TV, etc. They became good friends, met each other's families, and Virginia helped nurse David through hip surgery recovery. During the following year or so, they became very good friends and companions. By mid-2002, they came to realize that they truly loved each other and decided to become husband and wife. They realized that they could be happy and have a wonderful life together as long as the Lord should allow (particularly relative to David's health). They were married on January 11, 2003, at Mobberly Baptist Church among over 200 loved ones and friends. Their children served as their attendants. Virginia's dear friend from the Longview area, Elaine Pinkerton, was her Matron of Honor, and David's cousin and great friend since teenage years, Tommy Minter, flew in from California to be his Best Man. Tommy had also been David's Best Man for his first wedding. The newly-weds honeymooned on an Hawaiian cruise.

They sold Virginia's house in Pine Tree in the summer of 2003 and lived in David's house in Spring Hill until April of 2004, when they moved to "their" White Oak house—so that David could end up where he started out. Their White Oak house is less than a mile from the oil field lease where David grew up.

Virginia was born on April 24, 1938, and grew up on a farm southeast of Shreveport until about age 9 when her family moved to Shreveport. She has an older sister, Evelyn Bailiff, and an older brother, L. D. McGraw, and two younger brothers, Bill and Gene McGraw. Gene was a top executive for Texaco before his retirement.

Virginia graduated from C. E. Byrd High School in Shreveport and then attended Ayers Business College. She and Sam, a career Air Force gunnery radar technician, were married in December of 1956. They lived in Shreveport, South Carolina (where Sam grew up), Florida, Indiana, and Michigan before settling in Longview in the mid-1970's after Sam's retirement from the Air Force. Their son, Ron, was born in 1957, and their daughter, Julie, was born in 1959. Ron (with wife, Charlene, who is a dental office clerical manager) lives in Longview and works for an oil company. Julie (with husband, David Anderson, who works for FedEx) lives in North Richland Hills (Fort Worth) and is a medical lab manager. Virginia worked various clerical jobs, including civil service, while Sam was in the Air Force. After they moved to Longview, Virginia worked as office manager for Union Tank Car Company for 28 years. She officially retired the week of her and David's wedding.

Through her marriage to Sam, Virginia has four grandchildren and three great-grandchildren. Ron's children are Amanda Ouzts Mathis and Eric Ouzts. Julie's children are Lacey Pyle Talley and Chase Pyle. Lacey, an operating room assistant, and Brian have great-granddaughter, Haleigh, and great-grandson, Landyn. Amanda and Michael, both school teachers, have great-granddaughter, Emily.

Virginia and David enjoy traveling, especially cruising. It took more than a year to furnish and decorate their White Oak house and get the yard in shape, partly because they were "on the road" quite a bit. Virginia also sings in the Mobberly Baptist PraiSingers and enjoys reading and working puzzles. She loves beaches and the outdoors in general and in earlier years played golf, bowled, and square danced, and she is still a skillful, competitive athlete. In earlier years she was also actively involved in service in the military community and through Beta Sigma Phi, a ladies' sorority for social and service activities, and she received several awards and honors through these involvements. She is a great cook (especially of David's favorite foods such as meatloaf, beans, peas, and cornbread) and a neat, stylish housekeeper. Because of her nice figure, she also periodically models clothing in style shows for some of the local ladies' clothing stores. She is also a member of the select Red Hatters ladies' group.

David says that Virginia is a wonderful, fun wife. She supports and honors him and takes great care of him. Her attractive appearance and sharp intellect are important to him, but her kindness and compassion toward him and others is more important. Because of these traits, she is truly loved by David's children and grandchildren and by their many relatives and friends.

Below is a poem David wrote for Virginia for Christmas of 2002, a few weeks before their wedding, one he wrote for her on Mother's Day of 2005, and one he wrote for her as part of a fun, money gift at Christmas of 2007.

New Love, New Hope, and New Life

My first love was gone and my way seemed so bleak,
I prayed to the Lord, "What now should I seek?"
He told me to hang in, to have faith, to stay,
And soon there would come a much brighter day;

I went to the Garden to have a good meal
And there met a sweet doll and made her a deal,
We went to a party and then to the show,
And both of us wondered just where this would go;

We increased our dating, became best of friends,
We hardly could wait until the days' ends

When we'd grab a bite and then watch TV,
Or just sit and talk out under a tree;

Our families and friends all seemed to approve,
And we were determined not too fast to move,
But then it was clear that there was true love
Within this great friendship so blessed from above;

She's lovely and sharp, her touch is so dear,
It makes me feel good whenever she's near,
I'm proud when we're out because she's quite a "looker,"
And when we eat in, she's a wonderful "cooker;"

She says that she feels great love for me, too,
And that what we're sharing has brought hope anew,
So soon we'll take vows and become man and wife,
Because of new love, new hope, and new life.

> I love you, Virginia,
> Christmas 2002

My Love, Virginia,

I love you more as time goes by,
And here are a few of the reasons why—
When we disagree, you compromise,
And when I hurt, you sympathize;
You rub my foot, you hold my hand,
And when I goof, you understand;
Your kitchen talents bring me bliss
But not as much as your hug and kiss;
When you "doll up," you look just great,
And I'm so proud that you're my date;
But every minute you're my love,
You're like an angel from above;

You constantly light up my life,
And I'm so blessed that you're my wife.

> Love,
> David
> Mother's Day, 2005

A Christmas Gift for Virginia
(My Favorite Super Model)
Christmas 2006

I love you once ($), I love you twice ($),
I love you 'cause you're very nice ($),

I love your looks ($), I love your touch ($),
I love your cooking very much ($),

You are My Sweetheart ($) and Best Friend ($),
I'll love you to the very end ($),

So buy yourself some gems and clothes*,
'Cause what you want "me doesn't knows." ($)

> *Love ($),*
> *James David*

* Or whatever

Virginia normally spends a great deal of time finding just the right card for birthdays, anniversaries, etc., but then she usually adds a sweet note of her own. The following are a couple of David's favorite notes from her.

To My Wonderful Husband,

I can't begin to count all of the ways that I love you—the thoughtful things you do for me, the fun and happy times we share, and just being near you all make me thankful and proud that I am your wife. I love you for your quiet and patient strength, for the way you apply your talents and abilities, and for the many things you do for me and others.

You are my friend, my hero, my lover, my wonderful husband, and I am very blessed to be loved by you.

Love,
Virginia, 2006

My Dearest David,

My heart overflows with love for you on this Valentine's Day (and every day). I am truly blessed to have someone as special, loving, and caring as you for my "Valentine." I hope you never doubt that you are my hero, my best friend, and the one that makes me very happy. On this special day, know that you are my love and special Valentine forever.

Love,
Virginia
Valentine's Day 2007

2.3 DAUGHTER, MILLICENT "MILLI" LAUREE' ALEXANDER JACKS

David assures everyone that Milli was and is a dream daughter. She started out on August 30, 1968, as a beautiful infant and became more beautiful and lovely as the years passed.

Milli was always a hardworking "A" student and received most of the top awards throughout her prep school years. At the end of her high school career at Clear Creek High in the spring of 1986, she was the recipient of the Weber Award, given to the outstanding all-round student in the senior class. At that time Clear Creek High was one of the largest high schools in the state. Until (and including) 1986, there was only one recipient per year for this top award. Beginning the next year there was a male recipient and a female recipient.

Milli also received the following other top awards and honors: American Legion Award (female), Magna Cum Laude, Gold Medallion Award, All A's Honor Roll (all four years), Most Likely to Succeed, Most Dependable, Student

Body President, Outstanding Choir Member (female), All Regional Choir, Chamber Chorale, Top Tennis Player (female), Academic Scholarship to Baylor, and Representative to Lone Star Girls' State.

During her freshman year in high school, she wrote an original song entitled, "Look Me in the Eyes and Tell Me You Love Me," which advanced to and received Honorable Mention in a national contest.

Her high school principal, Ralph Parr, said near the end of Milli's senior year that he considered Milli to be the most outstanding student to come through Clear Creek High during all his years there.

Surprisingly, Milli dated very little during high school. She had a lot of good friends, male and female, but one-on-one the guys were apparently intimidated by her. Several guys later told Sandy and David that Milli was so beautiful and smart that they knew she wouldn't want to go out with them.

At Baylor, Milli continued to be a top student, academically and otherwise. She became a member of one of the top sororities, Pi Beta Phi, serving as vice president her senior year. She was selected as Outstanding Senior Woman, one of only ten to receive this honor. She received a Bachelor Degree in Business Management and Computers in May of 1990.

She was accepted into Baylor Law School in the spring of 1990 and actually began law school classes before she completed her final exams her senior year at Baylor University. She graduated in the top 20% of her law school class in February of 1993 and passed the Texas Bar Exam later that spring. She then worked as an attorney for about six years until she became pregnant with her first child.

Milli was married to David Lee Jacks in Beaumont, Texas, on June 15, 1996. Their first home was in Ft. Worth where David Lee was attending Southwestern Baptist Theological Seminary. He received a Master of Theology Degree in 1998, and they soon afterward opened a Christian bookstore called Theological Pursuits. On the evening of October 17, 2000, a few hours before Sandy passed away, David Lee Jacks II, David A.'s only grandson, was born. What a mixture of sadness and joy, especially for Milli.

At the time of the writing of this book, David II is age 6 but the size of a normal 8-9 year old. He appears to have a much higher that normal I. Q. and memory capability. He is reportedly the top student in his kindergarten class, a top performer in his karate group, plays the piano, and sings with David A.'s quartet on occasion.

Little sister, Laura Alexis, was born on September 29, 2002, and is now age 4. She is also very smart and talented. She has already begun to read and write and sing on tune. Plus, she is beautiful, looking much like Milli at that age. Granddaddy David needs to sew his buttons back on every time he thinks about any of his grandchildren.

Milli possesses the outward and inward beauty of Sandy but is also a lot like her dad. One of David's favorite aunts, Frankie "Sunshine" Alexander, suggested that "Milli has her mom's looks and her dad's look." Most folks might say that she inherited the best from both of her parents. She exhibits Sandy's compassion and affection and David's basic initiative and competitive spirit, and she is in some ways surprisingly athletic like David. She is a very generous giver of gifts and of her time. She is also a poet and a prolific song writer, having already written more than 100 songs.

Christmas of 1990 David gave to Milli a poem he wrote entitled, "To My Dream Daughter, Mil." It is presented below.

To My Dream Daughter, Mil

The first time I saw you I knew deep inside
That a great love between us would ever abide,
That a beautiful life that day had begun,
That my life would be blessed through this little one;

From the first time I held you to this very day
You've brought pride and joy to brighten my way;
Your awards and achievements are hard to believe,
Though I feel that the best ones you're yet to receive;

You're a sight to behold, your beauty is rare,
Seldom has there been a lovelier "Bear,"
But what's truly special about you, Precious Mil,
Is your capacity to love and your marvelous will;

You attract lovely friends, other "daughters" I claim,
Kristi, Caroline, and Merideth are a few I will name,
And one blissful day Mr. Right will appear—
I'd not be surprised if he's already near;

Yes, "Daddy's Little Girl" has grown up so fast,
And most of my dreams you've already surpassed,
So let me proclaim once more how I feel—
I love and adore you, My Dream Daughter Mil!

Love,
Dad

For David's 60th birthday in November of 1999, Milli presented to David a book of about 75 letters that she had collected from many of his dearest relatives and friends. She included in the book a poem she wrote to David, and it reads as follows:

Daddy, Daddy

Daddy, Daddy—you're so tall;
You're the "handsomest" of all!
Bulging muscles, eyes so blue,
Strength to always get you through.

Daddy, Dad—before I nap
May I sit upon your lap?
Cuddle oh so close to you?
Talk about my love for you?

Daddy, Daddy—help me pray;
I don't know quite what to say;
Get me started with a prayer,
Lots of things for me to share.

Daddy, Daddy—watch me play;
You can work some other day;
Watch me run and laugh aloud;
Hope to make you oh so proud.

Daddy, Daddy—watch me swing;
I can do most anything!

Watch me soar up to the sky,
High enough to almost fly.

Daddy, Daddy—hear my song;
I have practiced all day long;
Every line I sing for you,
Harmonize the whole way through.

Daddy, Daddy—as I ran,
Greeting you outside the van;
Home at last to end your day;
Now it's time for us to play.

Daddy, Daddy—I would plea—
One more hour of TV?
I'll be glad to rub your back
Just before we "hit the sack."

Daddy, Daddy—I would praise—
Tell me 'bout your "glory days,"
All the races you have won,
High school, college—oh what fun!

Daddy, Daddy—I would pout—
No one wants to take me out;
Is there something wrong with me?
Something that I do not see?

Daddy, Daddy—help me out—
Calculus is quite a bout;
Things I just don't understand;
Thanks for giving me a hand.

Daddy, Daddy—I would rave—
Look at all the money saved

From our all-day shopping spree,
Lots of clothes for Mom and me!

Daddy, Dad—I had a hunch
You'd come and pick me up for lunch;
Spiffy's or the yogurt place—
Lunch with Dad is just my pace.

Daddy, Daddy—here's a joke;
Don't repeat a word I spoke!
Thought it'd make you laugh a lot,
Funny words that hit the spot.

Daddy, Daddy—I must go
Off to Baylor—time to grow;
Learning, laughing, making friends,
Studying that never ends.

Daddy, Daddy—three more years
Competition with my peers;
Law school classes—stress galore,
Sleeping less but learning more.

Abba, Father—I would pray
Take my Daddy's hurt away;
Make his battered heart grow strong
So to praise You all day long.

Daddy, Daddy—I would smile—
Will you walk me down the aisle
To the one who loves me true,
Just the way you prayed he'd do.

Daddy, Daddy—Can't you see
You're the perfect Dad for me?

No one else could dare compare
To this Fox with silver hair.

Daddy, Daddy—You must know
How I truly love you so,
How you've filled my days with joy;
You're my hero—"Golden Boy!"

Love,
Milli

David wrote the following Valentine poem for Milli when she was age 6.

TO MY MILLI
(From Dad, Valentines Day, 1975)

My Precious Little Doll, the daughter of my dreams,
If I should love you more, my heart would burst, it seems;
You bring me so much joy and happiness and cheer—
If I could have my way, I'd have you always near.

You make me very proud because you act so nice
And try to do your best and listen to advice;
And though you treat me mean out on the tennis court,
You scratch my back so well, I forgive you, Little Sport.

The years are flying by and you're growing up so fast,
These special childhood days will soon be in the past;
So build your life on love, be thankful, and be glad,
And always know you're specially loved and cherished by your Dad.

In August before David II was born in October, Granddaddy David wrote a poem to him. With a few name changes, most of the poem would apply for any one of the other four grandchildren.

To Baby Alexander Jacks
From Gammy & Granddaddy Alexander
August 2000

Dear Baby Alexander Jacks, the time is drawing near
When through the miracle of life to us you will appear;
Our Lord will smile and with the angels we will praise His name;
Our hearts will overflow with joy—we'll never be the same.

Before too long you'll realize that you are truly blessed
To have a Mom and Dad that surely are among the best,
Whose lives are based on giving and integrity and love,
On faith in God because of grace sent down from up above.

Perhaps you'll be an athlete, one of the special stars;
Perhaps you'll be a scientist and help put man on Mars;
Perhaps you'll be a true hero and somehow find the ways
To help stop pain and hatred and brighten all our days.

As for your Gammy and Granddad, we hope you'll always know
That we'll be somewhere loving you wherever you may go;
You'll always be a part of us and we a part of you,
So be your best and make us proud in everything you do.

Love,

Gammy & Granddaddy

2.4 SON, DAVID GREGORY "GREG" ALEXANDER

Greg was born December 10, 1970. David finally had a son, and what a super son Greg has become. David also wrote a poem about Greg and gave it to him at Christmas of 1990. It is entitled, "To My Baby Boy, Greg," and is included at the end of this section.

Greg was selected as the Optimist Club's Student of the Year at the end of his eighth grade year, and later was selected as an Outstanding High School Student of America. He played football and tennis during junior high and part of his high school years and was an outstanding vocalist and instrumentalist throughout. He sang in the Chamber Chorale, the select vocal ensemble, for three years, and soloed the National Anthem for a football game or two.

It was obvious even when he was a little boy that Greg had a highly mechanical mind. As a 2-3 year old, he could change the toilet paper rolls and do other things with his hands that most children could not do until age 4-5.

He could also carry a tune from about age 3 and began singing with the family at age 4. He would sometimes say, "I'm not going to sing today," and Sandy or David would say, "Okay, you just sit here and wait while we sing." But the family never sang without him; he always changed his mind at the last minute.

On Christmas Eve of 2000, a little more than two months after Sandy passed away, Greg, Milli, and David sang in the Sunday evening service at Mobberly Baptist Church. Greg, with his wonderful voice, carried the group. They sang an acappella medley, and weeks later folks were still commenting on how much they had been blessed. It was a great Christmas gift from Greg and Milli to their dad, one of the best ever.

It was also obvious early on that Greg would be a computer and electronic genius. He had his first computer at about age 11, when he began writing his own computer games and other software. During his senior year in high school he worked as an apprentice for a NASA contractor, mainly involving computer software and networking. From there he never looked back and became one of the top computer specialists in the NASA area. He is now one of the most highly respected and highly paid people in his discipline, especially in his age range.

In 2001 he led in the development of computer software to allow the International Space Station astronauts while up in space to simulate Extra Vehicular Activities (work outside the spaceship) shortly before actually going out and doing the work. The software was placed on a CD along with a picture of Greg and his team. Greg later joked with David, "Well, Dad, you may have helped figure out how to put men on the moon, but I bet you never got your picture up in space."

Greg is also a leader in the music ministries of his church. He possesses much of his mom's natural music ability to play instruments.

He was married to Catherine Marie Duke Alexander on December 22, 1990, in Dickinson, Texas. Ali was born December 3, 1994, and passed away as the results of a car accident in late April of 1997. Caitlin was born June 19, 1998, and Megan was born April 7, 2000. Greg and Cathy are wonderful parents. At the time of the completion of this book, Caitlin and Megan are ages 9 and 7.

They are beautiful, sweet, and smart (top students), and they get along wonderfully with each other and with others. They both are very good swimmers, dancers, and karate students. They are a source of great joy to David. They spent their early years in the same house where Greg grew up because when David and Sandy retired and moved back to Longview, Greg and Cathy bought their house in League City. In 2003 Greg and Cathy bought a larger, beautiful house in a newer part of that same sub-division.

Cathy received a degree in music therapy from Sam Houston University in 2003. She and Greg now own a business called Harmony Lane Studios (named after Ali, whose first name was Harmony) involving Greg's computer science work (for which they have a subcontract from NASA) and Cathy's music therapy work. Cathy is also a pianist and vocal teacher and an outstanding vocalist.

Greg looks more like the Binghams (Sandy's family) than the Alexanders, but he is a lot like his dad in the way he loves and treats his wife and kids and in his sense of humor. He and Cathy have given some very special gifts in recent years to David and Virginia, including a big-screen TV, a huge entertainment center, and a stained-glass window (made by Greg), and Greg is always willing to help them with computer problems and questions.

To My "Baby Boy" Greg
Written by David for Greg—Christmas, 1990

The doctor came and said to me, "You have a baby boy;"
I yelled, "All right!"—then thanked the Lord, my heart was filled with joy;

Then through the years I seldom had to say to you "Behave,"
Though obviously I did forget to teach you how to shave;

You do not look a lot like me, and you may think that's fine,
But when you tell those corny jokes, I know for sure you're mine;

You've honored me at Barrios by all that you have done,
I'm always proud when folks find out that you're my handsome son;

And often times my pleasure's soared through special times we've shared,
Like when you've sung or played the bass or showed you really cared;

You've added to our family a very special one,

I hope her "other dad" I'll be, for my heart she has won;

And now, my former baby boy, you've grown into a man,
And I am glad to take the role as maybe your best fan;

I love you, and I hope the best in life you'll always see,
And that you'll always aim toward the best that you can be;

And though the future's never sure, there's one thing you can know,
A part of me will be with you wherever you may go.

Love,

Dad

Greg wrote a letter to his dad soon after Sandy passed away. The cherished letter read as follows:

DAD,

I HOPE THAT YOU KNOW HOW PROUD I AM OF YOU. THE WAY THAT YOU HELD YOURSELF TOGETHER AND TOOK CARE OF MOM WAS INCREDIBLE. I CAN'T IMAGINE WHAT LIFE WOULD BE LIKE WITHOUT CATHY. ALI'S DEATH WAS VERY DIFFICULT, BUT LOSING A WIFE WOULD FAR EXCEED ANYTHING THAT I HAVE EVER HAD TO ENDURE.

YOU ARE A MAN'S MAN AND I COUNT IT A BLESSING FROM GOD THAT YOU ARE NOT ONLY MY DAD BUT ALSO MY FRIEND. THE GIRLS ADORE YOU. CAITLIN IS ALWAYS TALKING ABOUT GRAND-DADDY. CATHY LOVES YOU MORE EACH DAY AS SHE IS EXPOSED TO THE PURE CHARACTER OF DAVID ALEXANDER.

I WANT TO BE AVAILABLE TO YOU. YOU HAVE ALWAYS BEEN THERE FOR ME IN HARD TIMES TO COMFORT AND REASSURE.

I LOVE YOU!

GREG

The following poem was written by David for Greg when Greg was age 4.

TO MY GREG

(From Dad, Valentines Day, 1975)

I love you David Gregory, My Little Tiger Man,
And always I will surely be your very special fan;
Someday you'll probably be a stud, so handsome and so tall,
And probably very talented and really on the ball;

For now you make me very proud when you act the way you should,
And when you smile and hug my neck, it makes me feel real good;
Some things you do so very well that I especially like
Are firing the coals, changing the rolls, and doing tricks on your bike.

You're growing fast and soon you will not be a little boy,
And yet I'll never forget the days when you were my "stinker toy;"
So grow big and strong, yet gentle and warm, and remember to love and give,
For only in loving and giving, My Son, will you learn to abundantly live.

2.5 FATHER, GEORGE WISEMAN ALEXANDER

David's father, George, was born March 26, 1906, and grew up on a farm in the hills of south-central Kentucky. He was the seventh among eleven children of Milton Elliott and Lee Ellen Barnes Alexander, whose families moved from Virginia to Kentucky in the early-1800's. Milton was a farmer, lumberjack, and oil field worker at various times.

George claimed that as a lad he walked three miles to school, uphill both ways, of course. He was the fastest runner around, although there were few if any organized sports in that area back then. As a youngster he came to Texas several times with his family to pick cotton. He, like most young people in that era, went to school only until the 9th or 10th grade. As a late teenager, he lived with an older brother, Fred (a World War I disabled veteran), in Colorado Springs, and then worked throughout the Central Plains for several years.

George came to East Texas during the oil field boom in the early 1930's, at about age 25. He was hired off the street as a roust-about by a company named Lucy Petroleum reportedly because he was tall and handsome and stood out in the crowd. He was still working for a branch of that same company 47 years later when he died on the job at age 72.

George met Olga, David's mother, soon after he came to East Texas in Old London, where she was helping her mother run a boarding house. They were married in 1931 and, about a year later, had a child, George, Jr., who died soon after birth. After trying unsuccessfully for about five years to have another child, they decided to adopt. In mid-June of 1938 they adopted Carolyn Elizabeth as an infant from the Gladney Home in Ft. Worth. Then about eight months later, Olga became pregnant with David. Before David was born, the George Alexanders moved to the oil field lease in north White Oak where David resided during his first 18 years. George was superintendent over the four Lucy Petroleum leases in the north end of the East Texas oil field. Having been raised on a farm, George normally planted a big, fine garden, and David grew up greatly enjoying plenty of home-grown vegetables. They also normally kept in a locker house in Longview plenty of beef usually purchased from the Gene Tevebaughs. Gene had come to East Texas with George during the early 1930's and ran a butcher house along with managing one of the Lucy Petroleum oil leases. He and George were great friends for many years.

George was a devout Christian and a man of strong convictions and high principles. He was a Baptist deacon, Bible teacher, and substitute song leader for most of his adult life. He never allowed alcoholic beverages of any kind or even playing cards in his house. However, he would play dominoes until midnight "because dominoes were not made to gamble with, and playing cards were." He was also very much against teenage dancing. He once interrupted a reception after a junior high football game, turned up the dimmed lights, and summoned Carolyn and David to leave with him. David says that the only serious disagreement he and George had after David was a young man involved whether David and Sandy (then just good friends) should help sponsor a back-to-college party and dance at a local community center. David was to be a senior at Baylor and Sandy a junior. After assuring George that older adults would be there and that the lights would not be dimmed, George finally halfway consented—which means that he didn't forbid.

But George was really a kind, fun, positive, charismatic, neat, clean-cut gentleman. Although he had a good sense of humor and loved jokes, he never told "dirty" jokes or used foul language. In fact, David assures that he never heard his dad curse or use profanity.

George was a natural athlete. Had he been born 20-30 years later, he probably would have become an outstanding high school athlete and possibly a college athlete. He was reportedly the best baseball pitcher in the East Texas oil field leagues. For sure, he hated to lose and was a solid competitor. Throughout David's junior high and high school career, George never missed one of David's games or meets, and seldom missed a practice. He attended quite a few of David's college athletic events, sometimes driving for hours to attend.

After David's final track meet at Baylor, when Baylor upset a highly-favored University of Texas team for the 1962 Southwest Conference Championship, George congratulated David with a firm handshake and said, "You saved the best 'till last."

Later that evening David and Sandy took George out to dinner and told him that they were in love and were planning to be married within a year. George was very pleased. He always treated Sandy as if she were the very best daughter-in-law he could have ever hoped for, which of course she was.

At the end of the summer before David's senior year at Baylor, he was selected to teach the Sunday School lesson in George's class as part of Youth Week. The lesson was about recognizing good Christian examples. David concluded by telling the class that his dad was the best Christian example he knew. David said that his goal was to someday be as great a man, father, citizen, and Christian as his father. Most of the men wiped tears away, and George seemed very pleased.

George often expressed great pride in David's athletic career as well as his space career. However, when David was a lad, George would say, "We'll never put men on the moon—if God had wanted men on the moon, He would have put them there Himself." He was probably as surprised as anyone when we did put men on the moon, and his own son was vitally involved in figuring out how to do it.

David will never forget something that George once told him. David had just discovered that his serious girlfriend had lied to him, and he was trying to decide if he should break up with her. He explained the situation to George, and George's reply was, "Son, you need to do what your heart tells you to do, but never forget that if you can't forgive, you can't love."

George passed away in November of 1978, when he was 72 and David was 37. When David, who then lived in the Houston NASA area, got to the funeral home in Longview, he asked to be left alone with his dad's body. As David sat down by the casket and began to weep, a vision came to him. He saw four young men, all about 20-25 years old, playing catch in a beautiful field. He realized that he was one of the young men and that his dad was another of the young men (because he had seen pictures of George when George was in his early 20's). It took a while, but David gradually realized that another of the 20-25 year-old young men was his son, Greg, who in real life was then not quite 8 years old. The fourth young man looked a lot like David and George, and finally it dawned on

David that it was his brother, George, Jr., who had died soon after birth. David remains convinced that he was shown a vision of the future in Heaven, where everyone will be at his or her prime physically and mentally, and everyone will be happy and having fun, in addition to praising the Lord.

A deacon friend said of George right after he died, "God never made a finer man than George Alexander." David certainly agrees and truly misses him. But George, George, Jr., Olga, Sandy, Ali, Sam, and all our deceased loved ones in the Lord are there praising God and waiting for the rest of us to join them.

2.6 MOTHER, OLGA MILDRED HOWETH ALEXANDER

Olga was born the oldest of three children to Marion Hampton and Flora Ann Hall Howeth and grew up on a farm about 10 miles east of Henderson, Texas. Her father died when she was 18 years old, and she and her family had some tough times during her later teens.

When people would comment that George must have been a good, natural athlete to have had such an athletic son, Olga, in her shy way, would say, "Well, I could outrun and out jump everyone in my class at school, including the boys." She was a good basketball player, and seemed to especially enjoy David's basketball playing when he was in high school. She reportedly was also the top student in her class academically, and according to the guys who grew up with her, one of the prettiest young ladies around. She had black hair and bright blue eyes. David says he can remember when he was 3-4 years old just wanting to continuously hug and kiss her because she was so pretty and sweet. Olga was a quiet, somewhat shy person, especially in a crowd or around strangers. However, one-on-one she was quite personable and an interesting conversationalist.

Olga was a wonderful mother to David. Like many moms in that generation, her main goal was to be the best mother and wife possible, and she gave most of her waking hours toward that end. Fortunately, she did not have to work outside the home while David was growing up. She made sure that David and sister, Carolyn, and George wore the nicest, cleanest clothes that they could afford, and that they had plenty of good food to eat. She was an ideal wife for George, supportive and submissive, as the Scriptures instruct.

She was an excellent cook, a perfectionist at sewing, and a constant encourager. Her cooking specialties were chicken fried steak, meatballs, meat loaf, garden vegetables, cornbread, and homemade fried pies. She made quite a few of

David's shirts when he was a tall, slim, fast-growing teenager "so that the sleeves would be long enough." She also crocheted very well and made crocheted bedspreads and afghans and other items for her loved ones.

The last few weeks before David left for California for his first job after college, he kept asking Olga to tell him how she made cornbread, but he stayed so busy that she could not stop him long enough to explain her recipe. Finally, the last night before he was to leave, he came home about midnight to find his mom waiting up for him. He asked her why she was still up, and she replied, "Well, I figure I'd better tell you how to make my cornbread tonight because we probably won't have time tomorrow." They went into the kitchen and she began, "You start with …, then you add a pinch of salt and a dab of sugar …" David interrupted, "Mom, what's a pinch and what's a dab?" Surprisingly, after he convinced his mom to give a bit more specific instructions, he did learn to make the cornbread,.

Olga had a pretty good singing voice and played the piano some. She made sure that Carolyn and David took piano lessons, which paid off for both but in different ways. Carolyn became an excellent pianist and organist, and David became a Gospel singer and composer.

Several years ago, David wrote the following about his mom and dad: "I tend to think of Mom and Dad not as old and wrinkled and bent (as they eventually became), but as they were when I was growing up—Dad, as he used to "knock fly balls to me" and as he led "There'll Be No Sorrows in Heaven" at the Sunday afternoon singings; Mom, as she looked in church when I was small and as she prepared those delicious meals when I could eat all day and not gain a pound. In any case, whenever and however I think of them, I always smile, if not on the outside, for sure on the inside."

2.7 SISTER, CAROLYN "CAT" ELIZABETH ALEXANDER CHANDLER AND FAMILY

David and Carolyn's parents, George and Olga, had a baby boy a year or so after they were married that they named George, Jr., but he died shortly after birth. After having no success at getting pregnant during the next 5-6 years, they decided to adopt a child. They adopted Carolyn (Cat) as an infant in June of 1938. Then eight months later Olga became pregnant with David. So Cat is about 17 months older than David and was two grades ahead of him in school.

Cat was an average student in school, but she was very talented as a musician, especially playing the piano and other keyboards. She began playing for church worship services at about age 12 and was a full-time church pianist for about 40 of the next 50 years, until health problems forced her retirement. She was also a secretary-office manager and taught piano lessons for many years.

Cat graduated from White Oak High School in May of 1956. After one semester at East Texas Baptist College, she married Mickey Meadows from Petersburg, Texas (near Lubbock) and moved with him to California to be a Navy wife. They parented two sons, Ken and David, but divorced after about five years. Carolyn later married Yank Gann, but he died of a heart attack only a few years later. After George died in 1978, Carolyn moved in with Olga and helped take care of her for about 15 years until Olga died in 1993. Cat met Jeff Chandler soon after Olga died, and they were married about three months later. David says that Jeff is like an angel that God sent to love and take care of Cat. This has become even more obvious since Cat broke her ankle in September of 2005. She has not been able to stand on it since and has been out of bed only sparingly. Fortunately, Jeff's niece, Tammy, has come to live with them, and she is able to care for Cat while Jeff is at work.

Ken and David Meadows both graduated from White Oak, married lovely young ladies, Debbie and Lorenda, and each couple gave Cat a granddaughter and a grandson. David's children, Emily and Daniel, have a daughter and son, respectively (Cat's great-grandchildren). Ken's children, Jennifer and Zackary, grew up in Tennessee and are both still single and pursuing higher education and vocational goals. Both Ken and David attended Sandy's memorial service and David and Virginia's wedding, Ken coming all the way from Tennessee.

For years Cat did a lot of research and documentation of the Alexander and Howeth family trees, which was greatly appreciated by both families. During her late-forties, Cat located her blood mother, Mary, and they enjoyed a great relationship for several years before Mary died. Olga was never told that Mary was Cat's blood mother.

Had it not been for Cat and her music talent, David probably never would have become involved in Gospel music singing and composing.

Cat used to travel all the way from White Oak to League City to keep Milli and Greg so that David and Sandy could go on weekend get-aways. David has often said that Cat's spirit has been an inspiration to him and many others. Years ago David wrote a poem about Cat, and it is included below.

My Cat

I have never cared much for birds or beasts
Or sneaky felines, to say the least,
Except for one sweet, soft, blue-eyed Cat
Who spreads special cheer "wherever she's at."

Her life has been far from a bed full of roses,
Much bad luck and sorrow her record exposes,
But seldom if ever will you hear her complain,
And her giving and loving are hard to explain.

She's been my prize Cat for many a year,
And our happy times have been many and dear,
Like singing together and hearing her play,
And answering the phone to her cheerful "Hey!"

Her love for my kiddos she couldn't show more,
And their feelings for her add up to "adore."
These verses are few but I hope they say this,
"I love very much this Cat that's my Sis."

Love,
"Little" Brother

Cat passed away on April 4, 2007, after the first draft of this book was sent to the publisher. The Four-Ever His quartet and the Alexander Family Singers sang at her funeral and graveside services. Cousin Jerry Alexander also presented the 23rd Psalms and David presented a brother's tribute (which included the above poem) at the funeral. Cat would have been very pleased.

3

Extended Family

3.1 PARENTS-IN-LAW

3.1.1 Sandy's Parents, Halton Elon (H. E.) "Bill" and Aline Gregory Bingham

H. E. was born in 1909 and grew up in Latch, Texas, but moved to White Oak with his parents as a teenager. Aline was born in 1916 in Central Texas but also moved to East Texas as a teenager. They were married in 1935 and made their home in White Oak for almost 60 years. H. E. worked for the railroad before becoming a Gregg County commissioner during the 1950's. He later served as mayor of White Oak, was a Mason and a member of the Lions Club. He was a shrewd businessman and made a great deal of money through real estate and oil investments. He was a big man, about 6'4" and 275 lbs (for many years). Aline claims that on their honeymoon, he stopped at a grocery store and bought a steak so large that she had to cook it in a large dish pan.

The Binghams were leaders in the White Oak Baptist Church. Aline was a member there for over 50 years and a Bible teacher for many years. She was also a leader in the White Oak School Parent Teachers' Organization when Janis and Sandy were in elementary school, and she was a super cook and homemaker.

H. E. and Aline were wonderful parents and parents-in-law, very loving and generous with their children, grandchildren, and families. They were highly-respected leaders in the community, giving generously of their time and other resources. In the late-1980's, they were selected as Mr. and Mrs. White Oak.

H. E. passed away in 1991 and Aline in 2002. David helped manage Aline's business and tax affairs after H. E. died, even during the last year or so of Aline's life after Sandy died. He regularly visited her in the nursing home and helped her eat her meals. After her Alzheimer Disease progressed to the stage that she could hardly speak, she continued to address David by his name whenever he visited her. The "in-law" really did not apply for their relationship, especially during the later years.

The world, especially White Oak, was and is a better place because of the Binghams.

3.1.2 Virginia's Parents, Pierce and Mary Farley McGraw

David never knew Virginia's father, Pierce, who died in the early-1970's. He was a farmer and then a baker after moving his family to Shreveport in the mid-1940's. He must have been a special person to have fathered and raised such sharp, successful children.

David did know Mary during the last couple of years of her life. During her earlier years, she reportedly was a wonderful mother and a special homemaker and seamstress. She was thrilled to tears when Virginia and David told her that they were getting married.

3.2 OTHER BINGHAM RELATIVES

3.2.1 Sister-in-Law, Rita Janis Bingham Canion and Family

Janis was about three years older than Sandy and was the means through which David became acquainted with the Bingham family. Janis was two grades ahead of David and three ahead of Sandy. During Janis' senior year at White Oak, she was elected Halloween Queen and needed an escort. She inherited her dad's tall genes and was six feet tall. David was about the only guy in high school taller than Janis that was not "going steady." So Janis asked David to be her escort, they became friends, and he became acquainted with the Bingham family.

A short time later, David won an essay contest about the importance of soil conservation. He ask Janis to attend the associated banquet with him. As part of the program, he read his essay, which began with the very "creative" sentence, "Soil conservation is very important." Janis and David still laugh about it. The essay judges were obviously a bunch of farmers, not literary people.

Janis is a Baylor grad (bachelor's degree) and later earned a master's degree. She taught English at Longview High School for about 15 years and then served as an administrator for 20 years, much of that time as Deputy Superintendent. She is one of the most respected and honored citizens in the Longview area. Among her honors are Star Over Longview and the Gregg County Heritage Award. She retired in the late-1990's but continues to serve on several community, education, and church committees. She does not yet have any grandchildren but treats David and Sandy's grandchildren (and children) as if they were her own.

She and Donnie Canion were married in the early-1960's. Donnie grew up southeast of San Antonio on a chicken farm. After they moved to East Texas, he worked in law enforcement and adult probation until he became disabled by a stroke in the late 1990's.

Janis and Donnie's son, Roger Bingham "Bing" Canion, is a White Oak grad. He was an All District linebacker at 160 lbs., and later in college developed himself into a 230-pound All Conference linebacker at Tarleton State. He is now Director of Juvenile Probation for Gregg County. Bing greatly loved and respected his Aunt Sandy. He gave her his college senior football jersey while she was fighting cancer in the mid-1980's.

Janis and Donnie and Bing have accepted Virginia and treated her with affection and respect. This is probably because David explained to them early on his relationship with Virginia—that although they began seeing each other about four months after Sandy passed away, their relationship remained primarily one of friendship and companionship for about a year after Sandy's death (see Section 2.2).

3.2.2 Sandy's Special Cousin, Betty Laura (& Gene King) and Family

Sandy's first cousin, Betty Laura Latch King, and her husband Gene King, and their children, Kristi and Brandon, were very special to Sandy and David. Betty is the daughter of Sandy's father's sister, Lola, and Gene was one of David's good friends while growing up and a high school teammate in three sports. Kristi and Brandon are very nearly the same ages of Milli and Greg, respectively. Unfortunately, all of the Kings have been reluctant to accept both Virginia and David's actions involving her. Although David explained to them the true situation involving his and Virginia's relationship (see last paragraph of Section 3.2.1), they apparently believe that David should have waited longer after Sandy's death before having a female companion in any capacity. David respects their feelings but hopes that their friendship will eventually be restored, and there are recent indications that such is possible.

When Sandy was alive, the Kings and Alexanders were like sisters and brothers. They spent a night or two together every time David and Sandy came to White Oak, and the Kings traveled to David and Sandy's many times, and they also took several vacations together. They were in each other's weddings and were always there for each other in bad times, like during serious medical problems and at funerals (parents, Ali's, Sandy's, and others). During a very sensitive time for Gene's family, David wrote a letter to his parents that they seemed to greatly appreciate. Whenever the Alexanders were visiting in White Oak, David often paid Lola a special visit while on one of his exercise walks.

3.3 DAVID'S FATHER'S RELATIVES

3.3.1 David's Alexander Grandparents, Milton Elliot and Lee Ellen Barnes Alexander

The Alexanders migrated in the early-1800's from Virginia to south central Kentucky where Milton was born in 1871. He met and married Lee Ellen when he was 22 and she was 16. Milton was a farmer, lumberjack, and oil field worker at various times. They moved to the Oklahoma City area in later years, and that is where David knew them as Grandpa and Grandma. They parented eleven children, and David's dad, George, was the middle child of the nine (six sons and three daughters) who grew to adulthood.

Grandpa was very hard of hearing in later years, and his blaring radio could be heard at night all around the area. He believed that photos were against Bible teachings and would not smile for a photo. He taught Sunday School at the Baptist church, although it was questionable if his doctrine was really Baptist.

Grandma Alexander was a very sweet-natured lady who seemed to never get upset. She was a "world champion" breakfast eater. She might eat 3,000 calories for breakfast and then not eat 500 calories the rest of the day. That could be one of the reasons why she lived so long.

David once told her that he thought she had the prettiest blue eyes he'd ever seen. She replied in her soft, sweet voice, "They're not any prettier than yours, Honey."

It was said of Milton and Lee Ellen that they never had much in material possessions because they would give whatever they had to anyone they thought might need it more than they.

3.3.2 Uncle Mike Alexander and Family

Mike was the first child of Milton and Lee Ellen and was a great patriot. He served in World War I, and when they would not let him reenter the military in World War II because of his age, he volunteered as a civil servant to support our troops and efforts in the Panama Canal region. He had two children, Billy and Barbara, by his first wife, who died when the children were young. He then married Frankie Copas, and had another son, Jerry. David and Jerry have become more like brothers in later years. He and his wife, Judy, are always there in time of need, like at Sandy's memorial service.

Of the six sons of Milton and Lee Ellen, only Mike and George had generic sons, and only Jerry and David had sons in the next generation. Jerry (and Judy) had three daughters (Jana, Brenda, and Kim) and one son, Mike, who has had a son, Ty, who is thus far the only "Alexander" left to carry on the Alexander name in the line of Milton and Lee Ellen. David's son, Greg, has had three daughters and probably will not try again for a son.

Billy (and Dorothy) had two beautiful daughters, one who was a beauty queen in college and who became a commentator for a national TV network. Barbara (and Red Dew) had two sharp daughters, Bunny and Debbie.

Jerry, an Oklahoma State grad, had a civil service career in forestry, and he retired in Russellville, Arkansas. His sharp, loving, and kind family is very special to David. His mother, Frankie, whom David nicknamed "Sunshine" because of her optimism and bright personality, turned age 102 in April of 2007. She and David have had a strong mutual admiration for each other most of David's life and have been long-distance prayer partners for many years. David wrote a poem for her in the mid-1980's about his realization that she often prayed for him. He wrote another poem for her and read it at her 100th birthday party . Both poems are presented below.

My Dear Sunshine
Written in the Mid-1980's
by David Alexander

The day began with a hectic pace,
Twas time again to join the race,
To help man travel toward the stars,
Back to the Moon, then maybe Mars.

Then driving down a crowded street
I felt a peace so sure and sweet;
My eyes glanced up toward the sky,
And there I saw the reason why;

For there above the rising sun
Appeared the face of a dear loved one,
And, oh, what glorious joy I felt
For I knew she at the altar knelt.

I saw her smile and speak my name,
His promises so boldly claim,
I heard her ask the Lord to bless,
Forgive, protect, and grant success.

I felt a tear roll down my cheek,
With heart so full I could not speak,
But my spirit said what she must know,
"My Dear Sunshine, I love you so."

Love,
David

To Frankie Gene Copas "Sunshine" Alexander
On Her 100th Birthday, April 3, 2005
by David Alexander, Nephew and Admirer

On the third day of April in 1905
A precious baby girl was suddenly alive.

She grew up a winner right from the start,
Became very special, so lovely and smart.

She earned her own way and got a degree,
Then taught many children their best to be.

She married dear Mike and brought him great joy
And gave them a sharp and wonderful boy.

Her grandchildren bless her, and we all agree
A more special friend there just couldn't be.

Her life has been filled with blessings and love,
And she gives all the praise to her Father above.

She's lived for a century, this lady so fine;
We thank you, Dear Frankie, for all the "sunshine."

Sunshine passed away on April 22, 2007, after the first draft of this book was sent to the publisher. As part of a tribute to her by David at her funeral service, he read the first of the above poems, My Dear Sunshine, and his original song that he had dedicated to her, Precious Lord, in My Heart I Love You, was played from the cassette tape of his first ten original songs.

3.3.3 Uncle Lewis Alexander and Family

Lewis lived to be almost 100 years old and was still teaching and preaching the Bible in his mid-90's. He farmed and worked in the Oklahoma oil field near Ada much of his life. He (and Olive) had two daughters, Grace and Kathryn. David seldom saw any of Lewis' family other than at family reunions. In later years, he was pleased to become better acquainted with one of Grace's daughters, Peggy (David's second cousin), and her family. Peggy, an American Airlines manager, and her sister, Mary, were both Texas All State basketball players at Southlake Carroll High School. Peggy and her David came to Sandy's memorial service and attend most of the family reunions as a representative of Uncle Lewis' family.

3.3.4 Aunt Eula Mae Alexander Yarger and Family

David referred to Eula as "my beautiful Aunt Eula," and he thought she should have been a movie star. She and George seemed to adore each other. Eula's husband of almost 70 years, Othel, was a fine, sharp gentleman. Their beautiful daughters, Anita and Celinda, are among David's favorite cousins. They and their husbands, Jack Fitzpatrick and Jerry Ferguson, and their children (Anita's Curtis and Renee and Celinda's Kim and Leesa, and their spouses) and grandchildren are David's special friends as well as relatives and are truly sources of family pride for David. Anita was an outstanding high school basketball player, and Celinda was (like David) a math major, and she became a high school math teacher. Eula and later Celinda (along with Cat) have done the main organizing for the Alexander family reunions through the years. Celinda and Jerry traveled ten hours (one way) to be at Ali's funeral and also traveled six hours to be at Sandy's memorial service.

3.3.5 Aunt Carrie Alexander

Carrie used to say, "Well, the right guy never came along at the right time, so I ended up an old maid." Her nieces and nephews became her children, and she definitely tried to spoil them. When David was 10-12 years old and his family went to Oklahoma City for a visit, David usually spent the night with Carrie. She had a hide-a-bed in her living room, and she would allow David to stay up and watch TV until he was ready to go to sleep. This was a special treat because the George Alexanders did not have a TV in those days. When David was in high school and college, Carrie drove many hours several times to watch him play football and run track.

3.3.6 Uncle Bob Alexander and Family

Bob, the baby of the family, was a World War II veteran and a self-made man. He developed a highly-successful swimming pool business in Corpus Christi, where his wife, Frances, grew up. They had three lovely daughters, Sherry, Dottie, and Robbie, who all married well (Chuck, Bo, and Bruce) and raised some sharp, talented children. Bruce was a college football player, and he and Robbie's two daughters became outstanding athletes, especially in basketball. The older daughter, Carey Beth, became the fourth descendant of Milton and Lee Ellen to make All State in Texas high school basketball. The others were Peggy and Mary O'Brien (Lewis' granddaughters), plus David. Bob himself was a good high school basketball player.

3.3.7 Other "Alexander" Relatives

David hardly knew most of his other "Alexander" relatives, seeing them only a few times in his life. Jimmy, George's brother, younger by a couple of years, lived in Corpus Christi and worked for an oil company. Some said that David actually looked more like Jimmy than George. Jimmy (and Inez) had a daughter, Shirley, and an adopted son, Butch.

Elizabeth Alexander Spann, George's older sister had four sons and two daughters, but they lived in Illinois and then Arizona, and David never saw any of them but 2-3 times. When David was headed to California for his first job out of college, he stopped in Phoenix to visit Aunt Lizzy (as everyone called her). One of her sons, Willis, Jr., also lived in Phoenix, and his wife, Jean, stopped by Lizzy's while David was there. When Jean started up the sidewalk, David stepped out onto the front porch. From about 40 feet away, Jean said, "Willis, what are you doing here? I thought you were at work." David said nothing but just stood there. When Jean got about 10 feet away, she said, "Oh, my gosh, you're not Willis, are you?" David introduced himself, and Jean insisted he have dinner with them that evening. Willis and David did look a lot alike for first cousins, although Willis was 10-12 years older.

Another of George's older brothers, Fred, was a World War I hero and was sick a lot during later years because of damage from poison gas during the war.

Milton's brother married Lee Ellen's sister, which resulted in several "double" first cousins that looked a lot alike. David has enjoyed becoming acquainted with some of his "double" third cousins at funerals and family reunions.

3.4 DAVID'S MOTHER'S RELATIVES

3.4.1 David's Howeth Grandparents, Marion Hampton and Flora Ann Hall Howeth

It is thought that the Howeths came originally from Germany (as Howets) through England to southeast Texas up to what is now Rusk County, Texas. The Halls supposedly came from the Deep South to East Texas. Hampton and Flora married in 1903, and David's mother, Olga, was born to them in 1904. They were farmers and owned hundreds of acres of land. Hampton died at age 41, when Olga was 18. He was diagnosed with heart disease, but in the early 1920's little was known about heart disease, especially coronary disease. Flora, with two younger other children, Ivy and Pauline, had a "tough row to hoe." When oil was discovered about 20 miles west of their farm, she opened a boarding house in the oil field at Old London. Olga met George there while helping Flora run the boarding house. Flora later returned to farming and ranching. She had a couple of failed marriages before marrying Luther Free, who was still there when she died in 1957. Flora was a tough lady, maybe an advocate for modern women's rights before her time. She was usually the only female at the cattle auctions and did work that normally only men did. She had three grandsons and five grand-daughters, and most would say that she was partial to the grandsons.

3.4.2 Cousin Louise Howeth Minter Erwin

Louise and Olga were first cousins although Louise was 18 years younger than Olga. They became reacquainted at the funeral of a relative in 1952 and discovered that they each had 12-year-old sons and lived only seven miles apart. A day or so later David and Tommy met and soon became best friends. Louise became a "second" mom to David, and she refers to David as her "other" son.

Jack Minter, Tommy's father, died in an auto accident in 1964, and Louise later married T. C. Erwin. She owned and operated a beauty shop for almost 35 years until almost age 80. She is one tough, but big-hearted lady—and makes the best cornbread in the world.

3.4.3 Cousin Tommy Earl Minter and Family

Tommy lived in Gladewater, only seven miles from White Oak, but he and David did not know each other existed until they were almost 13. They technically are third cousins (as their mothers are first cousins), but they became much more than cousins or even great friends, they became "brothers." Although they were competitors in high school in basketball and track, that only strengthened their friendship. They never played against each other in football because in those years Gladewater was in Class 3A and White Oak was in Class A, and Tommy did not play high school baseball. They did play summer baseball together on White Oak teams for a couple of years. They actually tied three times in track races in junior high and high school, although Tommy was normally slightly faster. David was probably slightly better in basketball and baseball, but Tommy had the edge in football and track.

They became teammates and roommates at Baylor. Tommy was a 4-year letterman in both football and track and then played pro football for two years. He was inducted into Baylor's Athletic Hall of Fame in 1999, and David was allowed to introduce him. The introduction speech presented by David is included below, and it further summarizes David and Tommy's relationship and some highlights of Tommy's sports career. Also included below is a cherished note that Tommy sent to David to be included in David's 60th birthday book.

David and Tommy were each other's Best Man in their first weddings, and Tommy flew in from California to be David's Best Man in David and Virginia's wedding.

Tommy fathered two lovely daughters, Amy and Tammy, through his first marriage to Louiann, a Gladewater girl. That marriage ended after about 14 years, and Tommy married Nancy a few years later, and they ended up in California with Tommy owning a car dealership. Their son, T. J., is indeed a source of pride for them and "Mama" Louise. Nancy, an elementary school teacher, is a highly-ranked amateur tennis player in her age group, and it appears that T. J. is heading toward stardom in sports. David is hoping that the Minters will move back to East Texas in the near future so that T. J. can attend high school in a smaller system like White Oak—and so that David and Tommy can spend their later years as neighbors or at least seeing each other as often as they wish, and so that Tommy can be near his mother in the twilight of her life.

Dave Alexander's Introduction of Tommy Minter as an Inductee into the Baylor University Athlete Hall of Fame

When I was 12 years old, my mother returned home to White Oak from a funeral where she had become reacquainted with a first cousin of hers who lived seven miles away in Gladewater and who also had a 12-year-old son. The next day I met this third cousin of mine, and we immediately became best friends. After five years of competing against each other in sports, Baylor gave us the opportunity to become teammates. Though our separate paths since college have not allowed us to be together nearly as much as we would like, our special friendship remains—and that's why it's my special privilege to introduce the next inductee.

Tommy Minter was an outstanding three-sport athlete (football, basketball, and track) at Gladewater and is still considered one of Gladewater High School's all-time best all-round athletes.

He came to Baylor on a football and track scholarship in the fall of 1958 and earned three varsity letters in each of these sports. In those days, freshmen could not compete in varsity sports.

Tommy started in football all three varsity years as a running back and a defensive back; in those days everyone played both offense and defense. During his last two years, he played in two bowl games, the exciting Gator Bowl against Florida in the fall of 1960; and a year later in the Gotham Bowl in which a 5-5 Baylor team soundly defeated previously undefeated Utah State.

After graduating from Baylor with a degree in business, Tommy played two years of pro football with Denver and Buffalo.

But it may be in track that Tommy Minter etched the most unforgettable place for himself in Baylor sport's history by his performance (as a sophomore) in Baylor's first ever track and field conference championship at Fort Worth in the spring of 1960. Although our young squad had some of the best relay teams in college track that spring, we were a big underdog to a much larger and deeper Texas team at the conference meet. But Tommy was a star among stars that day as our 13-man squad upset the Longhorns. He won the long jump, placed in both the 100 and 220, and ran a leg on the winning sprint relay. He then remained a vital part of Baylor's outstanding track program during his last two years.

Under the late, great Coach Jack Patterson, Baylor won outdoor track and field conference championships again in 1962 and 1963. Even though Baylor's track program has been outstanding for most of the 35 years since then, those three outdoor track and field conference championships in the early 1960's are the only ones ever won by Baylor.

Tommy is a great representative of this early-1960's championship track era, as well as one of Baylor's outstanding two-sport athletes.

Please welcome one of the world's truly nice and fun guys—and my best friend, Tommy Minter.

Dear David,

You are my best friend and just like a brother to me. We started a bond in junior high school. We did everything together from movies, church, and sleepovers. I will always remember your dad reading us the Bible when we got home from a sporting event or a movie. Those were special times we shared. We both loved sports and supported each other in everything we did. After high school we went to Baylor to become roommates and continue our special bond together.

David, you will always be my best friend. You have a special love for the Lord and a gentle way of treating everyone that comes in contact with you. I feel so fortunate to be a part of your life since we were young kids growing up together. My wish is that my son, T. J., will grow up to be just like you.

Love,
Tommy

3.4.4 Aunt Pauline Howeth Grubenman and Family

Pauline was Olga's younger sister by 5½ years. She was a fun person and more out-going than Olga. She married Ernest Grubenman, and they had one son, Kenneth, who became a top manager for Uncle Ben's Rice. Kenneth was about four years older than David, but David, as an early-teenager, would usually spend several nights during the summers with the Grubenman's in Longbranch, Texas. David, George, Kenneth, and Ernest played many highly-competitive croquet games during those years. David was a groomsman in Kenneth's (and Elizabeth's) wedding, "even though Kenneth was an Aggie." Pauline died in a fatal auto accident in mid-1969, a couple of months before men first landed on the Moon.

3.4.5 Other "Howeth" Relatives

Olga's brother, Ivy Howeth, had four daughters and one son. David got to know the two younger daughters, Frances and Barbara, and the son, Marion, fairly well during his pre-teen years, but has seen very little of them since then, essentially only at a few funerals and other events.

Eleanor Duran was a cousin of Olga, but David and others his age called her "Aunt" Eleanor. She and "Uncle" Malcolm never had children of their own, so they claimed David and several other youngsters as their kids. David and 2-3 others would spend several nights together at Eleanor and Malcolm's farm in Pine Hill, Texas, each summer. They would go to country singings/dances or play games half of the night at the farm. Eleanor would sometimes claim she was going to bed. Then a few minutes later a ghost would appear outside the window (Eleanor with a sheet over her). She was truly a fun lady—and a great cook.

Mager Hall was Olga's uncle, although he was only 8-9 years older than she. He owned a country store for many years, accumulated a lot of land which eventually involved gas royalties, and thereby amassed an estate worth about a million dollars. When he died in his early-90's, his wife and son had predeceased him, so he left his estate to his three surviving nieces, Olga being one of them. When Mager was living in a retirement home in later years, David, when visiting the Longview area, would take him to get ice cream. He was proud of the fact that his great-nephew worked for NASA. Mager had worked for Howard Hughes in Houston during his younger years.

4

Friends (alphabetically by last name within subgroups, unless noted otherwise)

Because the contents describing the friends below needed to be kept fairly concise, David has included primarily the first thoughts and memories that came to mind about each couple or individual, largely as they relate to him. When a friendship involves the children or overall family, such is indicated by a "(s)" at the end of the family name.

David greatly appreciated the presences of a large number of his friends, especially those who traveled long distances, at Ali's funeral, Sandy's memorial service, and his and Virginia's wedding. Such long-distance attendance is mentioned throughout the sections below and also is listed in Section 7.2 for Sandy's memorial service. However, it may not be mentioned for everyone who attended these events because some might not have signed the register or because of oversight, but please know that all attendance, local and long-distance, was greatly appreciated.

An asterisk (*) is included with the names of individuals who were known to be deceased at the time this book was completed.

4.1 BEST OF FRIENDS

(long-standing, much time spent together, many overnight visits, friendship usually includes children)

Sid & Frankie Alexander(s)—Sid and David first met as roommates at Texas Lone Star Boys' State in Austin, Texas, during the summer (1957) between their junior and senior years in high school. Sid was the representative from Killeen, and David was the rep from White Oak. They essentially lost touch until Sid transferred to Baylor in the fall of 1960. He walked-on and made the Baylor football team as a backup running back and place kicker. He and David were college roommates during David's senior year and have since referred to each other as "Roomie." Sid and Frankie (banker), who is also a Baylor grad and from Killeen, were married a few months after Sid served as a groomsman in David and Sandy's wedding. After Sid finished his Baylor degree, he went full-time with the Air Force. He later was a pilot for Continental Airlines, then worked for the Department of Transportation, and settled in Conroe, Texas. Sid and Frankie have two sons, Bo and Scott, and both were outstanding football linemen at Stephen F. Austin University. Sid and Frankie traveled many miles to attend Milli's wedding in Beaumont, and then to attend Sandy's memorial service in Longview.

Bob & Norma Culpepper(s)—David and Sandy knew Norma at Broadway Baptist Church in Houston before Bob came (from western Oklahoma) to work at NASA, and they introduced Bob to Norma. David and Bob were co-workers but also very good friends, more like brothers. At lunch they would often split a meal. In addition to his science background, Bob is also an ordained minister. He gave Greg his first job with Barrios and always treated Greg as if he were one of his own kids. Norma is a home economics teacher, and they have two daughters, Laura and Cynthia, and a son, Scott, who is a doctor. Bob was one of the speakers at Sandy's memorial service, and he and Norma attended David and Virginia's wedding. A cherished letter that Bob sent to David and Sandy a few months before Sandy died is presented below.

Dear Sandy and Dave,

If this sounds like a love letter, it is because we love you for the friendship and support you have provided to us over the 37 years that we have known you. You have been more than friends to us. You have been available when times were tough and we needed support and strength. You have been a shining light in the window for us to follow and find our way when all other lights were gone and you were the only beacon standing. We have loved you for your friendship over the years in words and deeds. We have seen you gallantly undergo pain and suffering and yet maintain the faith like no other couple we know.

If this sounds like a hate letter, it is because of our deep love for you. We have seen you suffer with pain and discomfort through the loss of family. We hate to see you go through the pain and suffering. You have always given God the glory and pulled through in a manner that only a spirit-filled Christian could have survived. The pain and suffering of difficult health challenges as well as physical challenges you have overcome with flying colors. You are a beacon of light that we have been able to use to find the real meaning of life and have shown the love of Christ through your strong will and understanding.

If this sounds like a thank you note, it is because we are thankful for the opportunity to see you raise two wonderful children in a world that has not been ideal for knowing how to adjust to the changing environment. Your children have been able to survive and become outstanding contributing adults to the society and environment they have been tempted with over the years. We thank you for the opportunity to have worked with both Milli and Greg. We have been around Greg more than Milli, but it is obvious that they have both grown and developed the skills and knowledge to survive the harsh environment and pressures presented before them. They have been model summer employees and have contributed greatly to the tasks provided them. Greg continues to be an exemplary employee and goes above and beyond the call of duty to support his ongoing tasks as well as to pitch in and pull faltering tasks out of the fire and get the customer satisfied as well as his employer.

If this sounds like a hurt letter, it is because it has pained us to see you and your family endure the loss of precious health as well as the loss of your first grandchild. What a tragedy and how through the Power of Christ you have been able to survive and still show the power of the living Christ in your words and deeds.

If this sounds like an appreciation letter, it is because we love the effort you have put forth to demonstrate the Life and Love of Christ through your music abilities and talents both in song and ministry to the world around you. You have shown the rock of salvation to us in times of need in our lives. You have always supported us when we were making decisions about our spiritual, personal, and career decisions. You have always shown complete support in all areas of our lives. Milli has always been a strong academic model that we would like for our children to follow. Greg is a phenomenal employee and has always carried his weight in any environment he has been assigned to support. He has corrected errors that were not his job, and he takes responsibility to support "fire drills" that have short turn around time. He goes the extra mile to respond to short high priority tasks and yet maintains a good rapport with his regular tasks. Milli has always excelled, and she will continue to excel as a parent and as a legal professional.

Don't ask me why I wrote this. I was up late one night and started this to put in words the thoughts about you and your family that were fleeting through my mind.

We love you and want to support you in any way we can. Please call and tell us of needs you have.

In Christ,
Bob and Norma Culpepper
6-21-2000

Paul & Carole Gilmore(s)—The Gilmores and Alexanders became dear friends when Paul was Minister of Music and Youth at Nassau Bay Baptist Church in the mid-1970's. They spent much time together and even vacationed together, nine of them in a small station wagon with the luggage on top. Paul later built a successful landscaping business in the Katy area. Their children, Michael and "Doll" Terry were the same ages as Milli and Greg, respectively, and their "little" David later started on Katy High School championship football teams as a 175-lb guard. Most of the other linemen in Class 5A outweighed him by 30-100 lbs. Carole, a school teacher, is a wonderful soprano soloist, and Paul sings especially well in his canary-yellow sport coat. They were among the Houston-area friends who attended Ali's funeral and Sandy's memorial service. Paul sent the following letter for David's 60th birthday book.

Dear David,

Many years ago, God was moving in my life in a very special way. I knew in my heart He was telling me to go into "full time" church music ministry. An opportunity became available at Nassau Bay Baptist Church. This was a spiritual door I really wanted to walk through. I felt very inadequate due to the fact that I lacked a degree from "The Seminary" and certainly didn't have a solo voice to lead singing. God paved the way by sending a very special man who believed and supported me as I entered this new ministry. That man was Dave Alexander.

Dave, I can never thank you enough for the loyalty and encouragement you gave me during this special time in my life. There are so many good memories: Milli with her crackers and water, Sandy with children's church, your divine plan for packing our luggage on top of my station wagon for the trips to Wimberly, those special clothes of the '70's, and special songs such as "I Am Satisfied" and "How Great Thou Art."

God has had His hand on you and your family in a way that truly glorifies His Kingdom.

God bless you on this special occasion.

Yours in the Faith,
Paul Gilmore and Family

Tommy & Paula Jankowski(s)—Paula and Sandy were suite-mates during their freshman year at Baylor. Paula later transferred to the University of Houston (her home town), but their friendship continued. When David and Sandy went to Houston right before their wedding to find an apartment, they stayed with Paula and Tommy. Their daughters, Stacey and Liesl, are a little older than Milli and Greg, but the Jankowskis and Alexanders were much like one family. Tommy owned a transportation business in Houston for years, and Paula taught math and then became head of the computer records for the entire Houston ISD. When it was found out that Sandy would need chemo treatments again after her cancer recurrence in 1997, she became terribly low. David called Paula and Tommy, and they arrived in Longview a few hours later, and Sandy's spirits were lifted tremendously. The Jankowskis, including Stacey and Liesl, were a tower of strength at Sandy's memorial service. Tommy is a big sports fan like David and was an outstanding high school athlete. He volunteered his services as the photographer for David and Virginia's wedding, and Paula served at the reception. They still visit several times a year, and David enjoys receiving Christmas cards from Stacey and Liesl with photos of their children. David wrote a poem for Paula and Tommy on their 25th wedding anniversary in 1987, and it's presented below.

<h2 align="center">Friends of the Best Kind</h2>
<h3 align="center">(To Honor Paula and Tommy on Their 25th Wedding Anniversary)</h3>

Dear Paula and Tommy, can it really be true
That 25 years have passed since your marriage was new?
And somehow can it possibly be about the same span
Since in bobby socks and flattops our great friendship began?

The memories are many and few of them sad,
So let's take a quick look at some great times we've had—
From the days of Royal Wayside and Telephone Road
To Spanish Village fajitas and the relaxation mode.

The cook-outs, the parties that lasted most of the night,
When our waistlines were slim, though we ate everything in sight,
The bridge and charades, we were all hard to beat,
But getting Stacey to bed was the most difficult feat.

Then along came new challenges—Liesl, Milli, and Greg,
But for family love and respect we've never had to beg;
We've helped them develop and been honored by the results,
And the Good Lord has blessed with four sharp young adults.

But let's not get too serious because that's just not our style,
For the symbol of our friendship is surely a smile—
Even through all the games that on brains are so taxing
Or when we just shoot the bull and spend hours relaxing.

Our vacations have been super, especially the cruise,
When the fun was near non-stop and little weight did we lose;
And why we're not rich, Tom and I just can't see,
Considering all the gals' savings on many a shopping spree.

Now let's not forget Gregory's and for sure not The Sting,
Nor the night at Carol's Kitchen and our Sound of Music fling,
Nor the trips to the river, oh what natural glamor,
Especially at Mayan—if only I'd had my camera.

There are other good reasons why our friendship's so swell,
All the Jans and Marie and Myrtle and Odell,
Plus all of the neat, special neighbors and friends—
It's really no wonder that the fun never ends.

Your home is a haven we have the pleasure of sharing,
Where we always feel welcome and know there's genuine caring,
Where the food's always great, and the gab's always free,
And one can even have fun throwing a ball at a tree.

Your marriage is so solid and reflects so much cheer
And love and other qualities that we all hold so dear;

Should we search the world over, I doubt we could find
Such warm, super people—friends of the best kind.

> Love,
> Dave, Sandy, Milli, & Greg
> February 1987

Paul & Phyllis LeBlanc(s)—The LeBlancs, from Thibodaux, Louisiana, and the Alexanders met at the Mayan Dude Ranch in Bandera, Texas, in the late-1970's and reunioned there for several years. Then Todd, their oldest son, died in a tragic accident, and they were so devastated that they greatly limited their activities for several years. Then in the late-1980's, they brought their youngest son, Troy, to Houston to visit the Johnson Space Center, and, at David's insistence, stayed with the Alexanders. A year or so later, David helped get Troy an intern job with Barrios. A separate section about Troy and his family is included in Section 4.2. During the 1990's, the LeBlancs and Alexanders traveled many miles to visit in each other's homes to keep their friendship strong. They came to Houston when Ali died and to Longview to Sandy's memorial service. Paul developed a highly successful insurance business and is being followed by middle son, Scott. Phyllis is a teacher at their (Catholic) church. She is also a gourmet cook, but probably doesn't weigh 100 lbs. The following is a note they sent to David on his 60th birthday.

Dear David,

You have touched our lives in many ways, and we have shared great joys as well as great sorrows. But what we love about you most, David, is your unshakable faith and commitment to your God and to your family and friends. Through the years we have felt and seen your strength, your courage, and your love, and through it all you have been the dearest of friends. Even more, you have been a model and an inspiration to us, and we are better people for it. You are, dear friend, a shining example of God's love. Thank you, and may your sixtieth birthday bring to you all the love and joy that you have brought to others.

> Love,
> Paul & Phyllis

Bill & Pat McCleary(s)—Bill is a Baylor tennis letterman, and he and David were fraternity brothers in APO (now SAE). After a few years as a sportswriter in Houston, he merged into the investment-insurance business and later became an advisor-agent for the Alexanders. Pat, also a Baylor grad, was an office-machine (typing, etc.) school teacher and is a great cook (especially potato salad). They settled in the Houston Woodlands area, where their son, Scott, was an outstanding high school basketball player. Bill and Pat are considerably more liberal than David in their theological beliefs, but that is not a problem for either. The McClearys don't just "talk" their beliefs, but they do a lot to improve the plight of the less-fortunate. They've always been there when needed, like when Ali died and at Sandy's memorial service, and for special occasions like David and Virginia's wedding. David wrote a poem for Bill's Big 5-0, and it's presented below.

Beyond The Big 5-0

I have a friend whom I call Billy Mac,
And up to now his wits have been in tact,
But now that he has hit the Big 5-0,
It's almost sure that something's gotta go;

Perhaps he'll start to lose his great physique,
And maybe low-cal foods he'll have to seek,
But with a super cooker like his Pat,
He simply may be destined to be fat.

His eyes may be the next thing to defect,
But thicker glasses may bring more respect,
And losing sight and sound should not alarm—
For Mocha will protect him from all harm;

Soon on the court to doubles he may switch,
And with a younger player he may hitch,
And if his back holds out and he endures,
You'll often hear him shout, "Yours! Yours!"

And what about the games at Baylor U—
Will he still tell the teams what they should do,
Or will he simply smile and tip his cap

And slip off to the Lounge to take a nap?

His Scott and Beth have made him mighty proud,
Their feats have often put him on a cloud,
And now that they have finally left the nest,
Just think of all that money to invest;

The TV, reading, Mocha, and the phone
Will still be there to turn "the old Bear" on,
But it will always be the best to share,
With family and friends who really care;

Well, thirty years and counting have gone by
Since I first came to know this "McBeary" guy—
I pray that he'll be blessed unto the end,
And that he'll always be my special friend.

Dave Alexander
April 1991

Dutch & Betty Lou Schroeder(s)—Dutch, a former pro baseball player, was a baseball coach at Baylor when David was an athlete there, but they didn't get to know each other well then. Dutch was a leader in raising funds for the "B" Association facility in the 1970's and then in managing its operation for over 30 years. During a track reunion hosted by the "B" Association in 1982, the Schroeders and Alexanders began their friendship, and during the next few years became dear friends. When Milli was a student at Baylor, Dutch and Betty Lou (high school P. E. teacher) were like extra parents to her. In the early-1990's, they rented a condo in Maui for a month each summer, and David and Sandy went over and spent a week with them a couple of times. Dutch coached a high school baseball state championship at Travis High in Austin and then coached Baylor to a share of a conference championship. He later became a P. E. professor. He is in the Baylor Sports Hall of Fame and has received several other top honors from Baylor. The walkway between the Baylor baseball and softball complexes is named for him. He was one of the speakers at Sandy's memorial service and also at David and Virginia's wedding rehearsal dinner. After David was inducted into the Baylor Letterwinners' Wall of Honor, the Longview News-Journal called Dutch to talk to him before publishing an article about the induction. Among other things, Dutch told the reporter that "David was one of the greatest men he'd ever known." In early-1994, David wrote a poem for Dutch's 70th birthday, and it was later read at several Baylor occasions, including Dutch's official retirement party given by Baylor.

DUTCH

by Dave Alexander (January 1994)

It all started out in Austin, Texas, in the winter of '24
When a neat little guy was sent down to Earth for Katherine and Emil to adore;
He quickly became a flash on the court and on the diamond he excelled,
A leader, achiever, to many a friend, near the top of the class he dwelled.

Three fine young brothers looked up to him as a model by which to live,
Then he answered the call and as a navy volunteer four years to
    his nation did give;
Then he left UT to become a Baylor Bear, with baseball stardom his fate,
And there Betty Lou slipped into his life, and he smartly made her his mate.

As a baseball pro he had some fun, then came Temple and Travis High,
Where he coached state champs amid the excitement of giving fatherhood a try,
Becky, Emily, and Tim arrived, the Schroeder saga to share,
Much joy and pride they brought to Dutch, but look what they did to his hair!

Then Baylor's brass brought Dutch back home to be the dugout czar,
And he led the Bears to much success and developed many a star;
But his greatest feats throughout the years, no doubt he'd surely say,
Are the many lives he's helped to mold and to show the Christian way.

His own grandkids now number seven, and they are quite a crew,
Eren, Hillary, Matt, Amanda, Jenny, Alex, and Savannah, too;
And his "adopted" kids may number a thousand, and he knows
    them all by name,
Via baseball, P. E., or otherwise, "One of Dutch's Kids" is their claim.

He's managed the Baylor Lettermen's Lounge since way back at the start,

And the way he handles its people and details is truly a special art;
He's one of the most distinguished and well-known men of Baylor U.,
To find someone who doesn't know Dutch indeed is hard to do.

With a great sense of humor, yet a sensitive spirit, a stranger he seldom meets,
But when a net's between, as in badminton or tennis, his opponent
    he usually defeats;
Fun vacations and healthy foods are things he seems to demand,
Plus an occasional trip to the storeroom frig for a spoonful of Eagle Brand.

He still finds time to lead at church and to spread the Holy Word,
And expressions of love and thanks to God from him are often heard;
And, believe it or not, he really does stop to relax ever once in a while,
Though doing and giving, not withdrawing or receiving, continue to be his style.

In 20-30 years from now when the old slugger flies away,
Thousands will wipe the tears from their eyes, and here's what you'll
    hear them say,
"He was truly a winner, a most-cherished friend, and he always came
    through in the clutch,
He brightened the lives of us and our kids, thank God for this hero
    named Dutch."

4.2 Very Special Friends

(long-standing, very special times together, usually get together if in each other's area)

David & Alexis Bennett—David Bennett was a track teammate (hurdler and sprinter) of David at Baylor, and is in the oil business in George West, Texas. The Davids have become closer during the last 15-20 years since Bennett became a solid Christian and a special encouragement to David A. He and Alexis traveled all the way from George West (between San Antonio and Corpus Christi) to be at Sandy's memorial service and at David and Virginia's wedding.

Dottie Cottingham—Dottie was an early teacher friend of Sandy who remained a dear friend of both David and Sandy throughout the years. She was the lead hostess for Sandy's baby shower before Milli was born, and is truly a fun person. She made the long trip to be at Sandy's memorial service. Her brother, Bucky Brandon, was a major league baseball pitcher.

Glynn & Betty Fields—Glynn was a year younger than David but a varsity track teammate at Baylor for two years. They ran on all three relays together but did not become special friends until later years. Glynn and Betty attended both Sandy's memorial service and David and Virginia's wedding. Glynn was inducted into Baylor's Hall of Fame the same evening that David was inducted to the Wall of Honor. Glynn is also in the State of Arkansas' Sports Hall of Fame.

Mike & Juanita Hackney(s)—Mike, from Canton, Texas, and David were competitors in high school football and track, and Mike then played football at SMU and became a dentist. In the late-1970's, the Hackney family (including children Michael, Joel, and Michelle) showed up at Nassau Bay Baptist Church on a Sunday evening because they were in town to visit the space center. David and Mike had not seen each other for about 20 years, and David did not recognize Mike when he greeted them. When David said, "Welcome, I'm David Alexander," Mike quickly replied, "From White Oak, right?" They fellowshipped at the Alexanders after church, David showed them around the space center the next day, and over the next few years they became special friends. The Hackneys own and operate some of the facilities at Canton's First Monday Trade Days, and whenever the Alexanders venture there, they have a good visit. They attended Sandy's memorial service.

Nancy & Misty (Miller) Jacks—Nancy is David Jacks I's mother and Misty his sister. They are Nana and Mimi to David II and Laura. David I's father, Jackie, died in the early-1990's, and Misty and her first husband divorced a few years later. In about 2002, Nancy and Misty moved from their original hometown of Beaumont to Fort Worth to be close to the David Jacks. Misty has found a special guy, Chuck Miller, and will be married by the time this book is published. Nancy and Misty are loving, fun ladies and always a pleasure to be around.

Howard & Mary Ann Jones & Gin—Howard began working at NASA while in the Air Force and continued as a NASA contractor after retiring from the Air Force. He and David worked together for several years. Daughter, Virginia (Gin), was a very good athlete in basketball, track, and speed walking, and David was an "advisor-coach" for her. Though a law school graduate, she is currently doing missions work in India, and David is one of her supporters. They all traveled from Houston to attend both Sandy's memorial service and David and Virginia's wedding.

Troy & Michelle LeBlanc—Troy is the youngest of three sons of Paul and Phyllis LeBlanc (see Section 4.1). David helped Troy get started at NASA, and

Troy has certainly proven himself worthy of David's efforts. He is now a highly-successful member of the NASA team. David composed a poem for Troy and Michelle (an attorney) and read it at their wedding rehearsal dinner in New Orleans, and they still call him "Mr. Dave." The poem is presented below. Troy and both of his brothers were top field goal kickers in high school. Troy briefs David once or twice a year about what's really happening in flight operations at NASA. In spite of Troy's busy NASA schedule, they traveled to Sandy's memorial service.

A Wedding Poem to Troy and Michelle

(Rehearsal Dinner, July 22, 1993)

The first time we met this young man named Troy, just a shy little lad was he,
'Twas the Mayan Dude Ranch in Bandera, Texas, but his potential even
      then one could see,
And the years since that time have yielded much evidence that he's
      something special indeed,
An achiever, a winner, with goals toward the sky, into the future he will lead;

The first time we met this doll named Michelle, she quickly won a place
      in our hearts,
Her sharp look, her sweet smile, and many other qualities that only pure
      beauty imparts,
At the top of the class, a leader, a friend, and also with goals very high,
There's really no doubt that with the best of legal eagles someday she
      surely will fly;

The time has now come to join in wedlock these two so perfectly matched,
An event so well-planned, so beautiful and proper, with joy and
      excitement attached,
With such parents and families and all these dear friends, few couples
      have e'er been so blessed,
And we're sure that in marriage, as in most other things, they'll score very
      high on the tests;

And now, if we may, a little advice that we hope will help on the way—
Dwell on the good, give and forgive, and often look upward and pray,
And never forget that honor and faith and attempts to make happy must be
Constantly part of a wonderful marriage, where love is natural and free;

So aim for the stars in love and in life and don't be confused by the crowd,
For your blessings give thanks, in your trials hang tough, and continue
     to make us all proud;

I'm sure that I speak for all of us here, even ones whom we cannot see—
From the deeps of our hearts we wish you the best, and we know that
     <u>the best you will be</u>!

Love,
Mr. Dave & Mrs. Sandy

Don & Elaine Pinkerton(s)—Virginia and Elaine became friends through a ladies' sorority soon after Virginia and Sam moved to Longview in the mid-1970's. Don and Sam were also great friends. Elaine was Virginia's Matron of Honor in David and Virginia's wedding. The Pinkertons have two beautiful daughters, Ann and Cindy, who are also friends of the Alexanders, as are several other Pinkerton relatives. The special get-togethers at the Pinkertons are always great fun.

Maxie* & Mae* Richards(s)—The Richards lived behind David and Sandy in League City for 15-20 years. They were 15-20 years older and were like an extra set of grandparents for Milli and Greg. They had two neat sons, Ronny and Tommy, who have remained friends of David. Maxie and Mae owned a large grocery store, and Maxie had a fancy inboard fishing boat. David went fishing with him mainly at the Galveston jetties periodically, and a delicious fish fry usually followed.

Roy & Ann Smalley(s)—Roy, from Greenville, Texas, was a track teammate of David at Baylor and one of the main reasons why Baylor won the conference championships in 1960 and 1962. The Smalleys and Alexanders have become closer friends after college years. Roy submitted the main nomination for David for the Baylor Letterwinners' Wall of Honor, to which David was selected in 2005. Roy should have already been selected for Baylor's Sports Hall of Fame (David has nominated him twice). He was a Marine and then in the auto repair and classic car restoration businesses, and he has had cars in several museums. They, with daughter Wendy (who is a brain cancer surviver), traveled to Sandy's memorial service.

Neal and Mary Alice Watkins(s)—Neal and David were fraternity brothers at Baylor. Then Neal served as the Alexanders' family doctor for about their last 20 years in League City (where Neal grew up). David would say, "It's great to have a brother for a doctor." The Watkins and Alexanders vacationed together several times. They made the trip to Sandy's memorial service.

Ken & Tricia Young—Ken and David were co-workers at NASA in the orbital and rendezvous planning area for many years, and Ken was David's supervisor for part of that time. They played together on several NASA league basketball and softball championship teams. Ken was about 6'6" and a good athlete, although he did not play sports at huge Austin High in Austin. Ken and Tricia, a real estate agent, both had children from their first marriages and then had a daughter from their marriage. Ken was one of the speakers for Sandy's memorial service. Ken and David each wrote poems for each other, and both are presented below.

Happy 60th, Ken Young, My Friend
(by Dave Alexander, June 1999)

The first time I saw him, he was skinny and tall,
And today he's still tall—but not skinny at all;

We hit it off quickly, in sports we were cool,
Especially when competing in the branch football pool;

We worked very hard to put men on the moon,
And to keep all the rendezvous stuff in tune;

It was NCC/NSR, toward the target to cruise,
Then CSI/CDH, Chris Kraft to confuse;

We'd go out to lunch when things got too tough,
Or head to the links to spend time in the rough;

On different orbits our careers finally flew,
But 'tis always a pleasure old times to renew;

Now Ken's turning 60, but I shall not cry,
I'm happy that someone is older than I;

All kidding aside, it's great just to know
A guy who is truly a NASA hero;

Without Ken the space race might not have been won,
For sure, it would not have been half as much fun;

When the words have been said and the songs have been sung,
This honor I'll claim—I'm a friend of Ken Young.

ALEXANDER THE GREAT
by Ken Young
2-16-90

Dave came out of Baylor with his slide-rule real handy,
With a degree in math/physics and a pretty wife named Sandy;
He started out with NASA way back in '63
Near Wayside and the Gulf Freeway at old H P C;

Dave's Apollo contributions are hard to overlook—
On lunar rendezvous he about wrote the book;
As an M-PAD engineer, he had quite a chronic wit—
When asked for rendezvous equations, he "threw a conic fit"!

A worker first and always, yet Dave also starred at sport,
We loved his baseline jumper—he was fluid on the court;
Few sports escaped his skills, but football was his real love—
On the field or in the "pools" he was just a cut above;

He helped build F D S while still in old M-PAD,
Then moved to M O D to help with the latest FADS;
As a resourceful manager, Dave pushed contracts from their blocks—
He helped pull one really big one up by its ST-SOCS!

Now, like some aging athletes, when they stop all their running,
One Day Dave got bad heart news, which indeed was quite stunning;
He had to change his lifestyle, especially his eating habits,
But slim, trim "Miss" Sandy taught him to eat much like the rabbits;

Then a bypass or three got him out of bad trouble—
With a big heart like Dave's, they had to do more than a double;

Yes, Dave's a true Christian, a deacon in the church,
But I hear a few years ago he had to make a big search—
Seems they wouldn't let "Uncle Dave sing in the choir—in the choir,"
So he just formed his own group with some singers he admired;
They're called The Master's Vessels and they really sing the Gospel,
And Dave's arrangements and originals are what make it all pos'ble;

But enough of this doggerel—just one more thing I'll state—
All this is why to me, you see, Dave's "ALEXANDER THE GREAT"!

4.3 SPECIAL FRIENDS

(present or past friendships with special meaning for various reasons)

Dallas & Nelda Anderson—Dallas was the second tenor in The Master's Vessels quartet during the entire 12½ years of their ministry, and he truly had a golden voice. He owned and operated a tree service/landscaping business. Nelda was quite good at introducing songs during the Master's Vessels' concerts and could be the life of the party. They traveled to Mr. Bingham's funeral, and Dallas sang at the graveside service.

Rick & Karen Anderson—Rick is the first tenor in the Four-Ever His quartet and works at Eastman in Longview, but he lives about 25 miles north of Longview near Diana, Texas. Although he is not currently a member at Mobberly Baptist, he grew up going to church there. His dad, Howard, is still a member at Mobberly and sings with David in two choirs and in the Men of Praise. Rick and Karen are both in their second marriage and together have five daughters from their first marriages. Below is a special verse David wrote for "I've Got a Feeling Everything's Gonna Be All Right," which the quartet sang at Rick's 50th surprise birthday party.

Rick's Special Birthday Verse for "I've Got a Feeling"
by Dave Alexander, March 10, 2007

A great big guy named Ricky could sing so high and sweet,
And when he met dear Karen, he swept her off her feet;
Now, he was quite a hugger and quite a ladies' man,
But he didn't know no better than to be an Aggie fan.

For Courtney, Ashley, Lacey, he's a father true,
And for Dusty and Sarai, he's a daddy, too;
Now soon he's turning 50 and must head the senior way,
But as he counts his blessings, I'm sure you'll hear him say—

Well, I've got a feeling everything's gonna be all right …

James* & Mim Blackwood(s)—The special relationships between the Alexanders and the Blackwoods (James & Mim, Jimmy & Mona, and James' nephew, Cecil) is expressed in the following article written by David and sent to the Southern Gospel Music Association in July of 1998. James passed away in early 2002, and Cecil, who managed and sang baritone for the Blackwood Brothers quartet for many years, passed away in 2001. James, who was in the Gospel music ministry for almost 70 years, was probably the most awarded Gospel singer ever and definitely one of the nicest, most genuine gentlemen ever. David was blessed to be able through the years to support financially and otherwise the ministries of the Blackwoods. During the last few months of Sandy's life, James called every week or two just to say that he and Mim were praying for Sandy and David at least twice every day. James sent a 60th birthday letter to David emphasizing to him that age 60 is not old, but that age 80 (James' age at that time) qualifies as old. Right after Sandy passed away, James sent a letter expressing his love and appreciation for Sandy and David, and Greg read the letter as part of his talk at Sandy's memorial service. David was sick with strep throat and was unable to attend James' funeral in Memphis, but he and Virginia attended a memorial concert in James' honor in Memphis a year or so later.

**Entry for "Share Your Story"
for the Southern Gospel Music Association Newsletter
The Impact of My Relationship with James Blackwood and Families**

(by Dave Alexander, 1998)

This is a story of how an encounter with first-class Southern Gospel music and a relationship with first-class Southern Gospel music people have affected my life and thereby the lives of many others.

I grew up in the East Texas oil field about 100 miles east of Dallas and was a top student and athlete at White Oak High School from where I graduated in 1958. I went to Baylor University on a football and track scholarship and earned a degree in math/physics. In early 1963 I began a 32-year career with NASA at the Johnson Space Center in Houston. I was vitally involved in putting men on the moon, in training the astronauts to perform space rendezvous, and in supporting the Apollo missions from the Mission Control Center. Later I helped design the Space Shuttle and its missions.

I grew up as a Baptist and was exposed to good "amateur" Southern Gospel music. In fact, I started singing in a mixed quartet at age 12. However, because of athletics and academics and later my space career, music was pushed into the background for about 25 years of my life.

By age 37 I had climbed high on the NASA management ladder, had a marvelous wife, Sandy, and two great kids, 8-year-old Milli and 6-year-old Greg. Life was busy but wonderful. Then I suddenly began having strange feelings in my chest and shoulders, was diagnosed as having advanced coronary heart disease, and was told that bypass surgery would be required. At that time coronary bypass surgery was relatively new and far from the perfected procedure it is today. My family and I were devastated.

About a week before my surgery was scheduled, some friends from our church invited us to go to a Gospel music concert at the Music Hall in downtown Houston. We arrived late and our seats were in the balcony. I don't remember much about the first half of the program, but I'll never forget what happened during the first song after the intermission. The Blackwood Brothers, featuring the great, late first tenor Pat Hoffmaster, reverently walked onto the stage and began singing "Blessed Assurance." Tears began to flow down my face and a glorious peace swept over me, and I knew that everything would be fine.

Soon after my surgery, I wrote to the Blackwoods and shared what had happened and expressed my appreciation for their ministry. The next time they were in the Houston area, Sandy and I attended their concert and went to eat with them afterward. During a later visit, I showed them through the space center, introduced them to some of my astronaut friends, and they came to our home for a meal before singing at our church that evening. We've since gotten together nearly every time any of them has been in East Texas.

But the story doesn't end there. Though I received several special awards from NASA for my technical and managerial contributions, my most cherished award is that of being selected in 1993 as Outstanding Citizen in the Johnson Space Center Community. One of the main reasons I received this award was because of my involvement in the Gospel music ministry via a part-time male quartet, The Master's Vessels. It was the Blackwoods who primarily inspired me to get back into Gospel music, resulting a few years later in my putting together, managing, and singing baritone for The Master's Vessels; Sandy was our pianist. We were together for over 12 years, averaged 45-50 engagements per year, and recorded seven albums, which include ten of my original compositions. It was truly an honor for us to sing on the program with James at a benefit for Pat Hoffmaster a month or so before Pat died. Most importantly, a number of folks were led to the Lord through our ministry and many others told us that our ministry inspired them to a closer relationship with the Lord, and to Him goes the praise and glory.

Our relationship with the Blackwoods has grown closer through the years, especially during the last few years. I had coronary bypass surgery for the second time in mid-1994 and, following the advice of my doctors, decided to retire in early 1995 at age 55, and we moved back to our original hometown (Longview) area. Sandy initially had breast cancer in 1986 but went almost ten years after treatment before it reoccurred in early 1997. She has been courageously fighting it ever since and has been on the Blackwoods' prayer lists through it all. James calls and writes periodically to assure us that he and Mim "call our names to the Lord at least twice daily." We also regularly pray for them because of the health problems James has experienced in recent years. Jimmy and Mona are also phone and prayer partners with us.

I consider it a tremendous honor to have the James Blackwoods as special friends. But who wouldn't? Anyone who knows anything about Gospel music knows that James is one of the most honored singers and most respected gentlemen ever in the Gospel music world, and Jimmy is following in his footsteps. And what lovely ladies are Mim and Mona. Though I don't know Billy personally, he obviously has become a wonderful Christian leader.

Thank God for the Blackwoods and may His blessings continue to flow down upon them.

Hal* & Pat Boone—Hal and Pat were among David's older friends (15-20 years older). Hal, who passed away in 2004, was a medical doctor who became a missionary doctor in Kenya, Africa. In the mid-1970's, he was critically injured in a land rover accident and was paralyzed from the chest down. As a paraplegic he served as interim pastor at Nassau Bay Baptist Church and later as Minister of Missions at Sagemont Baptist Church in southeast Houston. David and Sandy were members at each of these churches during the times Hal served at the churches. Hal, who is a Baylor grad, served on Baylor's Board of Regents for several years. Hal and Pat traveled to Beaumont so that Hal could lead a prayer at Milli's wedding, and they traveled to Longview to be at Sandy's memorial service. Pat has said on several occasions that she considered it an honor to be able to take care of her Godly husband. David says that she is not the singing Pat Boone, but the angel Pat Boone.

Les & Merideth Chambers—Merideth was one of Milli's roommates at Baylor, and remains one of Milli's dearest friends. Merideth's dad, Earl Wayne Miller, was a Baylor athlete a few years ahead of David. Merideth, who looks a lot like Milli, is like a daughter to David. Les, an attorney, and Merideth, a school teacher, live in Lufkin, Texas. After the car accident near Lufkin in which Ali died, Les spent several hours helping Greg (and David) with legal matters and would not allow Greg to pay him a penny. Merideth and Les were a tower of strength especially for Milli at Sandy's memorial service.

Bob & Linda*/Gay Doan—Linda and Sandy were great friends as co-teachers, and David and Bob became friends through the wives. Linda passed away in the early 1990's, and Bob later married Gay and moved to the Dallas area. They attended both Sandy's memorial service and David and Virginia's wedding.

Bill & Anita Durham—Bill became the bass singer in The Master's Vessels quartet when the original bass, David Leake, suddenly died in 1991. His first performance with the group was at the recording studio, as David Leake had died just before one of their recording projects was finished. Bill is a heart transplant recipient, and he was a college football player. He and Anita were at Sandy's memorial service.

Grover & Frances Gaskin—They are Virginia's aunt (and uncle) via Sam, whom she and Sam lived with for a short while in the early days. These great folks, accompanied by cousin Sandra Thomas, drove all the way from South Carolina to be at David and Virginia's wedding.

Tommy & Sherry Herndon—Tommy sings bass for the Four-Ever His quartet and is also an excellent solo performer. He owns a house repair business and is a house inspector. He was an All State football lineman at Spring Hill High School. He and Sherry met on a cruise after she heard him sing.

Pat* and Joann Hoffmaster—Pat was the incredible first tenor for the Blackwood Brothers in the 1970's and 1980's when they were among the very best of the Southern Gospel quartets, but he died from cancer in the early-1990's. David once gave Cecil Blackwood $100 to buy Pat a much-needed pair of new dress shoes, but asked Cecil not to tell Pat where the money had come from. Years later during the benefit for Pat right before his death, he smiled at David from his wheelchair and proclaimed as loudly as he could in his weakened condition, "I'm gonna be okay 'cause I got me a new pair of shoes." David and Joann became friends and email buddies after Pat's death, and David sent her several donations in Pat's name.

Jim Irwin*—Apollo 15 Astronaut Colonel Jim Irwin had heart surgery about a month prior to David's first heart surgery in 1977, and David ended up in the same hospital room. The nurses at St. Luke's told David that he reminded them of Jim. David had worked with Jim during the Apollo 15 planning, but they became friends later as they kept tabs on each other's heart condition. David spoke briefly at Jim's memorial service at Nassau Bay Baptist.

Mark & Anna Johnson(s)—Mark sings second tenor in the Four-Ever His quartet, is a banker, and has a lovely family. Anna is a school teacher, and daughter Lindsey and son Cooper usually give "Mr. Dave" a hug when their paths cross. Mark made a nice plaque for David containing a writeup about David's selection to the Baylor Wall of Honor.

Bob & Pat Kehl—Bob, a Baylor grad, shared an apartment with David in California when they both worked at the Naval Ordnance Lab before starting to work at NASA. They then worked together for several years at NASA before Bob started his own computer services business.

Jerry & Kathy Lanan—Kathy and Sandy taught together for several years before Kathy became an attorney. She occasionally presented sign language for some of the songs during The Master's Vessel's concerts. She and Jerry traveled from League City to attend Sandy's memorial service and then to attend David and Virginia's wedding even though they had a commitment back home and did not have time to stay for the wedding reception.

George & Carlee Marcom—George was the Alexander's family doctor for several years and lived across the street from them. As a young lady Carlee was a ballet dancer but gave it up to be a doctor's wife and to have four very smart children.

Neil & Pat Marshall—Before he retired, Neil was David and Sandy's family doctor the first five years after they retired and moved back to the Longview area, and he and Pat also became good friends with the Alexanders. He came to their house to check on Sandy (free of charge) the night Sandy died, and then attended her memorial service, which is unusual for a doctor. They enjoy Gospel music and have attended several Four-Ever His concerts.

David*/Wayne & Sue (Leake) Mitchell(s)—David Leake was the original bass for The Master's Vessels, and Sue did a beautiful job of presenting the sign language for some of their songs in later years. A couple of years after David died, Sue married Wayne Mitchell but remained part of the quartet group. The Master's Vessels, with replacement bass Bill Durham, sang at their wedding, and John Osteen, the original pastor of the great Lakewood Church in Houston, performed the wedding ceremony. The Leakes/Mitchells attended Lakewood Church, and the Master's Vessels sang there several times per year for several years. Sue and Wayne made the trip to attend Sandy's memorial service, and Sue signed Amazing Grace as it was sung by Thee Mobb Quad.

Earl Wayne & Carol Miller(s)—Earl is a Baylor football letterman and also played with the Green Bay Packers. He and Carol are the parents of Merideth, Milli's dear friend. They made the trip from McGregor to attend Sandy's memorial service. They were also fans of the Master's Vessels, and attended their concerts anytime the quartet was in the Central Texas area.

Virtie Miller*—Virtie was a co-resident and dear friend of Sandy's mother, Aline Bingham, at the Buckner retirement home in Longview. After Aline died, Virtie and David continued their friendship for several years until she passed away; he visited and had lunch with her periodically.

Don & Millie McLeod—The Alexanders met the McLeods from Fairfield, Texas, when The Master's Vessels sang there in the late-1980's. The McLeods opened their home for one of the quartet families to stay overnight, and the Alexanders were the ones to stay with them. They later traded visits several times through the years, especially when the Master's Vessels were involved. Don was a very good soloist and quartet bass but had a stroke in the early-2000's that partially disabled him.

Winnie Newman—Winnie is the owner and editor for the White Oak Independent newspaper and has been especially kind and receptive to David through the years. She supports and reports the White Oak community in an outstanding way.

Ware* & Bonnie* Phillips(s)—The Phillips were older and dear friends of the Alexanders. Ware was a Gospel music enthusiast and took David fishing on several occasions. Their two sons, Lowell and James Lynn, were teammates of David at White Oak.

Ross & Jennifer Rainwater—They are dear friends of Milli and David Jacks, and David has "adopted" them as his kids. Jennifer has a fantastic soprano solo voice and is willing to sing (especially at David's request) at almost anytime.

Ron & Donna Sanford(s)—Ron was the first tenor in The Master's Vessels and a college athlete like David. He and Donna were both school teachers/administrators and have two lovely daughters. They attended Sandy's memorial service.

Cody Terry & Family—Cody was a White Oak athlete in the late-1990's who reminded some old-timers of a young David. David advised and encouraged Cody through a few letters and became friends with his entire family. David led a prayer at the wedding of Cody's brother, Billy. They all, including parents, Steve and Susan, were an encouragement at Sandy's memorial service and at David and Virginia's wedding. Cody sent a letter for David's 60th birthday book, and David is not sure that he sent it to the right person. In any case, it's presented below.

Dear Dave,

The first I heard of you was from Coach Boyett when you entered the locker room and handed him the first letter I was to receive from you. He described the incident as you coming "out of the shadows, much like an angel." Well, though you weren't sent *straight* from Heaven, you have been somewhat of an angel to me, sent from God with encouragement in times I needed it most. You have proved to truly be a blessing to all you have come in contact with and an inspiration to those who have witnessed your life story.

Having read and studied about you and your past in White Oak books and papers, you have set a standard by which any White Oak student and athlete could be measured. Not only have you gained much respect in the classroom and on the court and field, most importantly, you have exemplified Christ in all you have done and humbled yourself in giving Him all the glory. As a role model to me, and only God knows who else, you have not only left a legacy for those of us behind you to follow, you are still living the legacy and never stop touching those around you. You are truly a hero, and I am blessed to have crossed your path, that I may be hopefully a small part in the making of your magnificent life.

It is written by an early American poet that one should strive to "either write something worth reading or live a life worth writing about." You have definitely lived a life worth writing about. You have excelled in all endeavors, showed the love of Christ in your actions and compassion for others, and have readily shared your faith in God to all those around you. How blessed your family must be for you to be a part of their lives, and how proud they must be, not just of your achievements and trophies, but by just being touched by Dave Alexander, the person and the Christian.

1 Corinthians 1: 4-9, Ecclesiastes 4: 9-12, Psalm 91: 11

Cody Terry

Caroline Walker and Family—Caroline was a roommate and dear friend of Milli at Baylor and is one of David's "adopted" daughters. Her parents, Charles (M.D.) and Pat Walker, invited Milli to live with them several months one summer when she interned at a Beaumont law firm, and then they would not accept any compensation.

Ed & Glenna Wandling—The Wandlings and Alexanders attended both Nassau Bay Baptist and Sagemont Church together. At Sagemont, Ed, Glenna, and David were three-fourths of a quartet, and Sandy was their pianist. Sandy and Glenna also led the music for the Sagemont children's church. Ed sang in the Houston Opera, and Glenna's brother's family, the Braschlers, have a theater and show in Branson, Missouri. The Wandlings were at both Sandy's memorial service and David and Virginia's wedding.

Winston Wolfe—Winston was a Baylor track teammate of David and later became a wealthy business owner in his hometown of Memphis, Tennessee, and a very generous contributor to Baylor. The field house at the Baylor track complex is named after him, and he was honored in 2006 as one of Baylor's top contributors. He invited David and Virginia to be his guest at the associated banquet, and he was a special guest at David's Wall of Honor induction.

Wayne & Pat Young(s)—The Youngs and Alexanders originally became friends at Nassau Bay Baptist. Wayne (PhD) was a top-level manager at the Johnson Space Center, and Pat was a piano teacher and church organist. David wrote poems for each of their three son's wedding rehearsal dinners, and Wayne and Pat were surprise attenders at David and Virginia's wedding. The poem that David wrote for the youngest Young son, also a "David," is presented below.

Ode to Dave and Trisha
(For Wedding Rehearsal Dinner, July 26, 1996)

by Dave Alexander

Tomorrow ere the sun shall set, the wedding bells shall chime,
And Dave and Trisha with hearts aglow shall start "their" place in time;
Their lives to date have known much love, great blessings and success,
But out ahead awaits a bliss mere words cannot express.

The Young and Mitchell genes in Dave have yielded quite a guy,
He followed both his brothers' steps as tops at Clear Creek High,
Then on to Baylor's hallowed halls the Green and Gold to fling,
With Sigma Chi, computer science, and pretty girls his thing.

Patricia Ann—we call her Trisha—is from the Plano tribe,
Though "plain old" one could never use this sweetheart to describe;
As history/education grad and Pi Phi Angel, too,
This special lady truly left her mark at Baylor U.

As Baylor Bears the two did meet and lit the flame of love,
Though they would part a while to wait the timing from above;
Then over in Austin, through a friend, their paths again would cross,
And they would know that they were meant to be "each other's boss."

So Dave gave up his traveling ways and got a job back home,
And Trisha agreed to move down where the giant mosquitoes roam;
But God will bless wherever they choose to blend their lives with Him
With joy and peace and lasting love whose glow will never dim.

Dave and Trisha, your future's bright and your dreams can all come true,
Through faith in God, to honor Him in all that you should do;
So now we join our hopes and prayers and wish to you the best,
And say to you, "Do all you can, and He will do the rest."

4.4 Special Coaches and Teachers

4.4.1 White Oak

Jack Blankenship—Junior high coach and teacher of David, and high school boys' tennis coach. He moved back to the Longview area a few years ago because he wanted to end up close to his former White Oak students.

Georgette Ellis*—David's math teacher, and David gives her credit for steering him toward a career in math and science. He wrote a letter to her in the early-1990's telling her that she had a part in putting men on the Moon because of her influence in his life. Her brother later told David that she had framed the letter and hung it in her living room. She drove herself from Shreveport to Sandy's memorial service, then had major surgery two days later during which she suffered a stroke and never recovered.

Emil* (& Vera*) Hanicak—David's basketball coach, coached two state championship teams (1953 & 1957), was small college All America at SFA, and is in Texas High School Coaches' and other Halls of Fame.

Alfred Lacy—David's science teacher; probably kept David from being Valedictorian—he gave only one test during one six-week period; David made 85 and everyone else made 20-30 points less; he curved all the other grades up 15-20 points but left David's grade at 85, which became David's grade for that six-week period; it was the only six-week grade David ever made below about 93; David later was edged out of Valedictorian by about 1 or 2 tenths of a point; but it really didn't ruin David's life, and he and Alfred are friends.

Bailey Marshall (PhD)—David's track coach and assistant football coach his senior year; coached state championship track team in 1958 and assisted in the coaching of the 1957 state co-champs in football. He later became Director of the Texas UIL.

Theo "Cotton" (& Lue) Miles(s)—David's football and baseball coach; coached the state co-championship football team in the fall of 1957. Later coached at Dallas' Woodrow Wilson and Skyline and is in Texas High School Coaches' and other Halls of Fame. A book was written about him in the late-1990's, and David was featured in one of the book's chapters. In his retirement, Cotton, a World War II vet, fishes several times per week. They traveled to Sandy's memorial service and David and Virginia's wedding.

Herman "Moon" (& Mary Jo) Mullins(s)—David's track coach and assistant football coach through his junior year and coached state championship mile relay team in 1957. He also was David's junior high basketball coach where he helped David develop important fundamentals. Moon, a World War II vet, is a Gospel singer and a Baptist deacon. As a teenager, David hoped he would some-day marry a lady as pretty as Mary Jo. They attended Sandy's memorial service.

Bob (& Mildred) Peery(s)—Junior high coach and then shop teacher of David. He later became school counselor and photographer. He was a World War II hero and his story was featured on TV after David told the TV people about him. On David's 60th birthday, Bob sent a very special note to David, and it is presented below.

Dear David,

I wish you a very happy 60th birthday.

David, having observed White Oak sports for 51 years, I consider you to be the best all-round athlete White Oak ever produced and also one of the best all-round students. It is a rarity to have a student that excelled in sports and academics and had a successful career and still be humble and courteous and have a deep faith in God.

Hope to see you on your 65th.

Love,
Bob Peery

Wesley Whatley—David's history teacher, who was also a fan of David's sports activities and was a bit partial to David when it came to grading; he was also a champion pistol marksman.

4.4.2 Baylor

P. D. Brown* (PhD)—Math and religion professor and always encouraging.

Bob Packard (PhD)—Head of physics department and helped show David around during his recruiting trip to Baylor. Milli also took a physics course under him.

Jack* (& Lois) Patterson—David's legendary track coach, coached Baylor's only three outdoor track & field conference championship teams in Baylor's history (1960, 1962, 1963), coached several championship teams at Texas, then came back to Baylor as athletic director for nine years. He was one of the best 400 hurdlers in the nation as a trackman at Rice in the late-1930's, and is a member of several Halls of Fame as both an athlete and a coach. A poem David wrote in honor of Coach "Pat" is presented in Section 1.4.3.1.

Walter Williams* (PhD)—Head of math department who tended to give David a few breaks because he (Walter) had run track at Baylor in the 1920's.

Kyle Yates* (PhD)—Religion professor at Baylor, after serving as one of the most respected Southern Baptist pastor for many years. Helped write the New American Standard Version of the Bible.

4.5 SPECIAL TEAMMATES

4.5.1 White Oak

William Athey ('59)—State Championship teammate and All Century in football (OL).

Buddy Baker* ('55)—Senior QB when David was a freshman; threw David's first high school touchdown reception to him; also teammate in basketball and baseball.

Sid Bratton ('55)—Outstanding senior lineman in football David's freshman year.

Dewayne Bruce ('57)—State Championship teammate in basketball; also football teammate, and outstanding tennis player.

Roy Bruce* ('59)—State Championship teammate in football, basketball, and track, and All State and All Century in football (RB); also baseball teammate; college football at TCU; died in auto accident in 1959.

Jimmy Cobb* ('55)—Teammate in all four sports David's freshman year; All State and All Century in football (E).

Mike Cobb ('57)—State Championship teammate in basketball and track (mile relay); All State, All Star, and All Century in both football (OL) and basketball (C/F, selected as All Star); also outstanding baseball teammate; college football at Baylor.

Jimmy Cox ('59)—State Championship teammate in football and basketball, and All Century in both; All State and All Star in basketball; also very good tennis player.

Jerry "Coon Eye" Davis ('59)—State Championship teammate in football, basketball, and track, and All Star and All Century in football (QB); also baseball teammate; college football at TCU.

"Old" Jerry Davis ('56)—Basketball teammate; married one of David's favorite classmates, Pat Greer; was referred to as "Old" Jerry Davis because of the other Jerry Davis who was three years younger.

Gene Gary ('58)—State Championship teammate in basketball.

Bobby Green ('55)—Teammate in football and track David's freshman year.

Mack Griffin ('59)—State Championship teammate in football, basketball, and track.

Jim Huggins ('49)—Teammate only on All Century football team (OL), but he was one of David's heroes and a neighbor when he was in high school, and they later became friends; Jim played college football at Tulane. In the late-1990's, David sent a history book about White Oak sports to Jim and told Jim he wanted to give the book to him because he had been one of David's childhood heroes; Jim responded by writing a poem about David and the incident, and the poem is presented below.

God's Gift of Love Your Pay

> By James Ebb Huggins, Jr.
> For Dave Alexander, 1999

Did you ever consider that you might be,
A hero to someone you've not taken time to see?
That how you act and what you do and say,
Might inspire an unknown someone and influence their way?

This happened to me many years ago,
When I was in high school, much energy to show;
I was proud and confident that I was among the best,
And did not take time to consider the rest.

As the years went by I was content with my gait,
And did not consider the effect I had on other's fate,
Until a short while ago when I met this special man,
Nine years my junior, from the same school we ran.

I did not recall him, he was little then,
But he said he remembered me and the other men
Who influenced his actions, swayed his way,
Caused him to persevere, caused him to stay.

He became a star athlete in high school, college, and more,
In physics and mathematics disciplines he did soar,

To become a NASA scientist, one who planned trips to the Moon,
One of our nation's heroes who won the space race, not a bit too soon.

As we corresponded, I asked him what did he spend
For a history book of our old school that he did send;
He said, "You owe me nothing for the copy, nothing to show,
It's my pleasure and the price I pay for a childhood hero."

I was humbled by his comment and very pleased too,
To think that I might have been a small part of what he would do;
So always think of others and watch what you do and say,
For you may be a childhood hero—God's gift of love your pay.

Gene King ('58)—State Championship teammate in football and basketball; All State and All Century in football (C); also outstanding baseball teammate; see also Section 3.2.2.

Marvin King* ('55)—Teammate in all four sports David's freshman year; great baseball pitcher; became ace of pitching staff at SMU.

Leon Lassiter ('57)—Teammate in football and track.

Travis McLane ('56)—Teammate in football; at about 225 lbs, was called "Big'un" during high school, but now weighs about 185.

Punk Miller* ('57)—Teammate in football; All State and All Century in football (OL).

Charles Moore ('57)—Teammate in football and track; college football at Houston; came from Dallas to attend Sandy's memorial service.

Pat Parrish ('58)—State Championship teammate in football; All State and All Century in football (OL); also teammate in baseball, and East Texas Golden Gloves boxing champion.

Lowell Phillips ('57)—State Championship teammate in basketball and track (mile relay); also football and baseball teammate; college football QB at SMU.

Edwin Roberson ('55)—Teammate in all four sports David's freshman year; All State and All Century in football (LB); college football at SFA.

Joe Lee Smith ('57)—Baseball teammate; later well-known, Hall of Fame sportswriter and statistician and led in the selection of White Oak's All Century football and basketball teams; probably knows as much about White Oak sports (especially the first 50 years) as anyone; has said that based on David's total athletic career accomplishments and honors, he could possibly be considered the best all-round "high school" athlete in White Oak's history, for sure among the top 4 or 5 (and probably the fastest).

Jerry Starr ('57)—Football and track teammate.

Billy Stites ('56)—Teammate in football (QB), basketball, and baseball; threw many passes to David his sophomore year.

Freddie Sutton ('59)—State Championship teammate in football, basketball, and track; in wheelchair since 1970's because of fall at work.

Geno Vaughn ('57)—State Championship teammate in basketball; also teammate in football.

Bob Wayt ('58)—State Championship teammate in football, basketball, and track; All State in football, and All Century in football and basketball; he and David are only Texas high school athletes ever to "start" on state championship teams in each football, basketball, and track; also baseball teammate; college football at Rice.

4.5.2 Baylor

David Bennett ('62)—Southwest Conference (SWC) championship track teammate in 1960 & 1962; see also Section 4.2.

Ronny Bull ('62)—Football teammate, All American (RB), and NFL Rookie of the Year; also Baylor Sports Hall of Fame

Eddie Curtis ('62)—SWC championship track teammate in 1960 & 1962.

Glynn Fields ('63)—SWC championship track teammate in 1962; Baylor Sports Hall of Fame; see also section 4.2.

Larry Harbour ('62)—SWC championship track teammate in 1960 & 1962; traveled from Dallas to attend Sandy's memorial service.

David Hawkins ('61)—SWC championship track teammate in 1960.

Billy Hollis ('60)—SWC championship track teammate in 1960; team captain.

Bill Kemp* ('63)—SWC championship track teammate in1962.

Tommy Minter ('62)—SWC championship track teammate in 1960 & 1962; also football teammate; Baylor Sports Hall of Fame; see also Section 3.4.3.

Bobby Ply ('62)—Football teammate (QB); later All AFL DB.

Bill Porter* ('63)—SWC championship track teammate in1962.

Burr Porter* ('62)—Football teammate and roommate junior year; the top student in Business School and later a PhD.

Marvin Sapaugh ('63)—SWC championship track teammate in 1962; once bought a large framed picture of Baylor's Pat Neff Hall at an auction where David's quartet sang and then gave the picture to David.

Roy Smalley ('62)—SWC championship track teammate in 1960 & 1962; team captain; see also Section 4.2.

Ronnie Stanley ('62)—Football teammate (QB); record-setting passer; threw David's first college touchdown to him; became a medical doctor.

Joe Thompson* ('62)—SWC championship track teammate in 1960 & 1962; became an attorney but died in late-1990's; his wife, Sylvia, and David still communicate.

Buddy Tyner ('61)—SWC championship track teammate in 1960.

4.6 "Girlfriends" (Approximately in Chronological Order with Maiden Name Listed)

Dixie Fisher—First "girlfriend" at age 5-6; also dated a few times in high school; remain good friends, and parents were also special friends of David.

Nancy Hall—Dated some in pre-teens and early-teens; parents were good friends of David. Her dad was one of David's memorable Sunday School teachers.

Janice Martin—Taught David "how to kiss" when he was about 12 although she was 2-3 years older; were in quartet together at Spring Hill Baptist Church.

Shirley Epperson—Dated in eighth grade; very pretty girl, but she moved away with her parents, and David loss track of her.

Karen Duran—Dated a few times in high school and a few times in college; remain good friends; she was from Gaston, Texas, and one of "Aunt Eleanor's kids."

Kay Penick—Dated some in high school, mainly to banquets and other special events; remain good friends.

Martha "Mot" Parten—Mainly doubled-dated with David's sister; remain good friends.

Gail Rambo—Mainly doubled-dated with David's sister; remain good friends; she was a Spring Hill girl.

Diana Duke—Met at get-together of Boys' State and Girls' State in Austin in 1957; corresponded throughout senior year in high school, and she went to Baylor, but things didn't work out mainly because of Cherry, next girlfriend on list.

Cherry Hanicak—Serious sweetheart during David's senior year in high school and first two years in college, but she ended up going to SFA, and things didn't work out. At White Oak she was Valedictorian of Class of 1960, cheerleader, and good athlete.

Nancy Nail*—Dated some as a junior at Baylor; she was from Mart, Texas, and was beautiful but a bit different; died in auto accident in mid-1960's.

Zelda Morris—Dated as a senior at Baylor; she was from Arp, Texas, and was pretty but a bit different; David was dating her when he fell in love with Sandy; see also Section 2.1 (third paragraph).

David dated 15-20 other young ladies a time or two each during his high school and college years, but the ones listed above were the special ones that he now remembers.

4.7 OTHER SPECIAL CLASSMATES AND SCHOOLMATES

4.7.1 Girls

Grace McMullin Blanton ('58)—State champion tennis player (doubles); cheerleader.

Joed Stites Brady ('58)—Drum major; still lives in White Oak.

Royce Toler Butler ('57)—Cheerleader; yearbook editor; manages reunions.

Pat Greer Davis ('58)—Co-student council officer; about 4'9" and she and David used to dance together.

Jimmye Looper Ferrell ('56)—State champion tennis player (doubles); cheerleader; went to Baylor; as CPA, helps David and Cat with income tax questions.

Shirley Davis Goss ('58)—Class Valedictorian; still lives in White Oak.

Shirley Rogers King ('58)—Cheerleader; All Round (with David) on Senior Hall of Fame.

Nona Roark Stansell ('57)—Drum Major, Most Beautiful, Miss Gregg County nominee.

Judy Thompson Shavers ('58)—Drum Major, Most Beautiful; Miss Gregg County.

Shirley Smith Manning ('58)—Good tennis player; sister of Joe Lee Smith.

Judy Allison Stuart ('59)—Drum Major, Most Beautiful.

Sue Huntley Yoder ('59)—Majorette; helped coordinate Sandy's memorial service and reception.

Pat Young Daniels ('59)—Cheerleader with Sandy; went to Baylor.

4.7.2 Guys

Pete Ferris ('58)—Moved away freshman year, but was good buddy in earlier years.

Fred Roberson ('58)—Moved away freshman year, but was good buddy in earlier years; still returns for most White Oak homecomings.

Jimmy Wilkins ('58)—Moved away freshman year, but was good buddy in earlier years; still returns for most White Oak homecomings.

4.8 OTHER PRESENT AND PAST FRIENDS

4.8.1 Other Mobberly Baptist Church Friends

Bob & Derrith Bondurant—Derrith is a beautiful, multi-talented lady, and Bob is a truly nice guy, and they are among David's younger friends (15-20 years younger). Derrith sang the Sandi Patti arrangement of "How Great Thou Art" at Sandy's memorial service and received a long, standing ovation. She sang "Eternal Life" at David and Virginia's wedding.

Carl & Winnie Breckel—They were also Spring Hill neighbors of David and Sandy for a while and often had the Alexanders over for family get-togethers and great meals.

Cindy Freeman—In David's opinion, Cindy possesses one of the most beautiful soprano voices anywhere. She sang "We Shall Behold Him" at Sandy's memorial service and will hopefully sing the two-verse National Anthem at David's memorial service.

Jack & Debbie Goetz—Debbie is a great church pianist and also plays for several ensembles. She played for Sandy's memorial service. Jack is in Classic Praise and Men of Praise (with David) and a golf pro.

Laney & Emily Johnson—Laney is both a great preacher and a great pastor. He has been pastor at Mobberly Baptist since the early-1970's and has four degrees. He officiated both Sandy's memorial service and David and Virginia's wedding. Emily is a sweetheart and a wonderful pastor's wife. They made the trip to League City to be at Ali's funeral. Below is a poem David wrote and read at the 30th anniversary of their being at Mobberly Baptist.

Truly the Best

From Goose Creek to Linden you became a bright star,
Since you answered God's call, your glow has beamed far;
Through ETB, Baylor, Southwestern, and more,
Your credits are many, your degrees number four.

You married a sweetheart, a lady so fine,
Then fathered two winners, the top of the line;
They and your grandchildren honor you so,
And your love will enhance them wherever they go.

With your smarts and drive, you could have succeeded
In most any field in which you'd proceeded,
But thank God, you chose to answer His call
And to stay the course—what a blessing for all.

You've led and inspired many thousands of us,
As a pastor and friend, you've earned an A+,
And as for your preaching, you rank very high—
With Sunday, Graham, and Silva, at least you would tie.

Your special delivery is truly unique,
As salvation or renewal you urge all to seek;
During your best sermons, folks often weep,
And anytime you're preaching, it's quite hard to sleep!

Your wonderful life is an honor to God,
And to Him goes the praise for the path you have trod,
For the lives you have touched and the souls you have won,

For what you have said and what you have done.

You've served our blessed Mobberly for thirty great years,
You've shared in our joy and also our tears,
You've shown us the way, your faith's stood the tests,
With Emily beside you, you're truly the best.

By Dave Alexander (April 16, 2000)
Written in honor of Laney & Emily's
30th Anniversary at Mobberly Baptist

Roger Johnson—Former IRS agent who is always willing to help David with IRS questions.

Thomas & Doris Moore—Both of them are White Oak grads. Doris "Ann" is a talented musician and a hugging buddy.

Kent & Sandy Mullikin—Kent is the director of the senior choir and in Cedar Creek (outstanding bluegrass group) and Men of Praise. He was a college football player.

Keith & Paula Parker—Keith, an A&M and pro football player, volunteered to handle the ushering at Sandy's memorial service, and Paula is a hugging buddy.

Dale & Shirley Perkins(s)—Dale, one of David's heroes, is recognized throughout the land as one of the great Ministers of Music. He has been at Mobberly Baptist since the late-1960's and has developed a tremendous music program. He was a speaker at both Sandy's memorial service and David and Virginia's wedding. He and Shirley also made the trip to League City to be at Ali's funeral. They and their five children and their families are blessings and inspirations to David. Below is a poem written and read by David on their 30th anniversary at Mobberly Baptist.

God's Music Man
A Tribute to Reverent Dale Perkins on His 30th Anniversary as Minister of Music at Mobberly Baptist Church

This poem's about a musician named Dale
Who teaches the "oo's" and the "ah's" so well,

And also when to soften or swell,
But seldom allows a breathing spell.

It all started out one Halloween
When his golden voice was just a scream,
But his parents' eyes showed a special gleam,
For of the crop he'd become the cream.

His early years were filled with sport,
A Louisiana hero was he on the court,
And on the gridiron a touchdown sort,
Why, few could match this guy's report.

And then he met his high school flame,
From a rival school sweet Shirley came,
And since then nothing's been the same,
So surely Shirley's his claim to fame.

Their early years were like a chase,
Houston, Corpus, and some Oakie place,
Then seminary days full of God's grace,
With tots to raise, twas quite a pace.

Then Mobberly called and wouldn't take "No,"
And God said, "Longview's the place to go,"
And through the years He's blessed them so,
Even given them lots of land to mow.

And what great kids, two dolls, three guys,
With mates and talents aiding spiritual highs,
And 17 super grandkids, in which much pride lies,
And even good answers to most of their "why's."

Plus wonderful friends to brighten each day,
Like Laney and Emily to help lead the way,

And so many more there's not room to say,
And even a few.... who love to eat hay.

Yes, horses and ranching are favorite things,
Plus to hunt or fish so much pleasure brings
To this modest man whose smile always sings,
And cheerful encouragement from him ever springs.

With a choir and office full of Debbie's and Peg,
For talent and advice he'll never have to beg,
But without them would be like ham without egg,
And without dear Clay, take an arm and a leg.

The choir has such talent it's hard to believe—
A blessing is there for all to receive;
When the ladies stop talking, which is hard to achieve,
Several so brightly to "high C" can cleave.

And those special groups just cannot be beat,
Whether guys, dolls, or mixed, or bells so sweet,
And when orchestra joins, that's Dale's favorite treat,
Along with bright ties and good food to eat.

Yes, the Pineville kid has come a long way,
And there's so much more that we might say,
But let's start an end to this poetic play
By wishing a Wonderful Anniversary Day.

Yes, Lord, it indeed has been thirty great years
That Dale's made us smile and inspired us to tears
And led us to You in times of great fears
And been a true friend that each one endears.

We praise You, Dear Lord, for sending this man
And sharing your love through him and his clan,

For blessing our lives through this marvelous span,

For blending our talents as only he, through You, can.

Written by Dave Alexander, a friend and admirer

From all at Mobberly Baptist who love and

appreciate Dale Perkins

September 1997

Bill & Bonita Presson—They had David and Virginia to their home soon after the Alexanders were married, and they are a very sweet, neat couple. Bonita usually takes Virginia to lunch for her birthday.

Leroy & Nancy Van Dyke—They were the first to have David and Virginia as a couple to their home, and that will remain special to the Alexanders. The following is a short poem David wrote for their 50th wedding anniversary book and celebration.

To Nancy & Leroy
On Their 50th Wedding Anniversary
(by Dave Alexander)

You helped get us started at the Garden that day,

Then you've made us feel special in your lovely way;

Your home was the first to welcome us in,

And we still can't believe that you let us win.

When you're not at church, the void is large,

For no one can match the way you take charge;

In creating beauty, you both have the touch—

We cherish your friendship for we love you much!

Other Mobberly Baptist friends (listed alphabetically by last name) are Sonya & Boyce Alexander, Howard & Betty Anderson, Paul & Floy Barber, Bob & Sylvia Bolding, Lynn & Dodie Bourdon, Delbert & Jean Bright, Randy & Janie Cape, Roy & Kay Chappell, Paul & Cristie Coleman, Alan & Pauline Conley, Raymond & Pat Curry, John & B. J. Dalton, Jim & Lou Davis, Brenda (& son Garrett) Day, Bill & Jerri Edmonds, Johnny & Sharon Gathright, David & Deborah Gilbert, Bob & Betty Gilley, Dora Gough, Don & Margie Gregory, Wayne

& Marian Hare, Rex & Thelma Haskins, John & Lessie Hawkins, Henry & Sherry Henderson, Milt & Opal Herzog, Roger & Debbie Kuykendall, Tommy & Sherry Lawrence, Jim Maxwell, Nathan & Linda McAllister, Bobbie & Bill McAlpin, Jack & Gail McDowell, Earl & Eva Mock, Rokky & Alisha Mullikin, Freda Nelson, Joe & Cindy Parnell, Gene & Shirley Petty, Charles & Alice Phillips, Scott & Cheryl Schulik, Jimmy & Terri Skeen, Del & Clara Smith, Jack & Wanda Reeves, Chip & Carole Rye, Don & Esther Satcher, Jack & Carolyn Thompson, Leo & Sandra Wall, Loren & Jean* Wells, Marvin & Sherry Williamson, Ed & Helen Wooldridge, Leroy & Peggy Worsham, Roger & Sue Wright, Greg & Tina Zackary, John Zenter.

4.8.2 White Oak Good Neighbors and Other Longview-Area Friends

Duane & Gena Childress(s)—Helpful neighbors on right.

Rick & Mary Crow(s)—Children of Breckels who were especially nice to David after Sandy died; David "adopted" their three daughters.

John Paul & Barbarah Dowell(s)—David's and Barbarah's families go way back; parents of former Miss Texas, Dana Dowell.

Jack Hale—White Oak ISD superintendent and counselor; very good vocalist.

Becky Hendrix—Favorite waitress (works at Red Lobster).

Bob Hoffer—Old Gospel music buddy.

Robbie & Cathy Huckaby—Special neighbors down the street.

James & Sue King—Near end of David's senior year at White Oak, James, then a freshman, gave David a graduation gift "to thank David for his example." James probably had to do without something in order to give the gift. One doesn't forget about such things. Sue's parents, E. B. & Claudia Carrington, were leaders in the White Oak schools and community for many years, and the White Oak High School gym is named after E. B. James is Marvin and Gene King's younger brother.

Rollin & Allison Kinwig—Helpful neighbors on left.

Bret & Stephanie McKinney—Young neighbors and real estate person (Stephanie), and daughter of builder, Rob Thompson.

Mickey & Dessie Meadows—Cat's first husband and father of their children; still good friends.

Theo & Mary Lou Meissner—She was David's first piano teacher and was pianist at White Oak Baptist for about 50 years.

Leon & Joann Pinkerton—Good White Oak friends; brother of Don Pinkerton; Leon was an outstanding high school football player at Lufkin.

David & Annette Sledge—Original bass singer for Thee Mobb Quad (that became Four-Ever His); played football at Oklahoma and survived severe wounds in Vietnam.

Cary & Arlee Small(s)—Were David's neighbors in Spring Hill; David helped coach their son, Ryan, in summer baseball.

George & Michelle Stone(s)—White Oak and Mobberly Baptist friends; teenage daughter, Brittany, has exceptional singing voice and is one of David's "adopted" kids.

James & Christine Tramel—Christine and David began special friendship as teenagers.

Tom & Deborah Wait & Families—David became acquainted with the Waits primarily through their two older children, Erin and Eric. Both are among White Oak's all-time best all-round athletes. Upon graduation from White Oak, both received the Alexander Education Foundation Scholarship, Erin (to Baylor) in 2004, and Eric (to LeTourneau) in 2006. Both are planning to become medical doctors. The Wait's relatives, the Carrs, are also special, talented people and friends of David.

James & Jena Wayt—Jena sang a duet with Chip Rye, "I've Just Seen Jesus," at Sandy's memorial service. James also sang in Men of Praise with David for several years.

Russell & Pat Wayt—The Wayts are outstanding White Oak citizens, involved in community and school organizations, particularly the education foundation. Russell was one of the great all-round White Oak athletes and then was a Rice and Dallas Cowboy linebacker. The Wayt's Christmas reception is enjoyed by many each year.

4.8.3 Other Nassau Bay Baptist Church Friends

Don & Trisha Carnes—They were friends in the small share group from church. Don wrote a poem for David's 40th birthday celebration, which is included in Section 7.7.

Sparky Chance—Sparky, a NASA employee, served with Sandy in the Nassau Bay Baptist Children's Church for several years. He moved to Tyler in later years and attended both Sandy's memorial service and David and Virginia's wedding. His nickname, Sparky, truly fits his personality.

Les & Susan Derrick(s)—Les and Susan were in the small share group with David and Sandy while they were members at Nassau Bay Baptist. Les was a High School All American runningback in Houston and then an outstanding runningback at Texas in the mid-1960's. He and David shared a bond because of their athletic backgrounds and their Christian service.

Gene & Judy Easley(s)—Judy and Sandy were co-teachers in the Nassau Bay Baptist Pre-School for several years, and Gene (PhD) became a top NASA administrator. Their two sons were good musicians, the older one an opera singer. They traveled from Houston to attend Sandy's memorial service.

David Jackson—A preacher boy in the mid-1970's for whom David and Sandy bought a suit, and he reportedly wore it for several years every time he preached. He and his one wife had a dozen generic children.

Jim Markgraf—The bass singer in one of David's church quartets in the mid-1970's who claimed he didn't know one note from the other, but he had a nice, very low voice. He was as strong as an ox, but a nice guy who was the definition of a die-hard democrat. David wrote a short poem for him soon before he was to re-married in the late-1970's, and it's included below.

A POEM FOR A LOW-DOWN FRIEND
(Prior to His Marriage and Move, Summer 1978)
By Dave Alexander

I have a good friend who's as strong as an ox,
A modern-day Sampson, with invisible locks;
He eats, works, and sings in a powerful style,
And his ways with the women bring many a smile.

If I were to guess at his favorite thing,
I'd say Jackie, or babies, or a low note to sing;
He can sing a "low C" in a mighty fine way,
But as far as he knows, he is singing a "K."

He moved up toward Dallas a good while ago,
But his heart stayed down here until, wouldn't you know,
He found him a sweet, pretty doll off up there,
Who apparently likes men with invisible hair.

We wish them the best, their children and all,

And we know that our friendships surely won't stall;

We're full of much joy for this special, new love,

And we pray for rich blessings on them from above.

Wyman* & Mel Mitchell—"Mitch" was Minister of Music and Youth at Nassau Bay Baptist during the 1960's when the choir was one of the better small choirs (40-50) in the Houston area. Half of the choir members were accomplished soloists. Mitch was like a coach and full of fun.

Bob & Kitty Millard(s)—Kitty (from Katy), a Baylor grad, was director of the Nassau Bay Baptist Pre-School when Sandy taught there and Milli and Greg attended there. Gentleman Bob was in the Strategic Air Command and then with IBM. Sons, Mike and Richard (and Richard's wife, Emi), are also friends.

Larry* & Ruth McLemore(s)—Larry was a big country boy from the Canton area, and he and David quickly became friends. They were in the small share group. Larry had three heart surgeries, and the last was an experimental one. As a State Farm supervisor, he and Ruth and their two sons moved several times through the years, but remained in touch.

Larry & Sharon Reel(s)—They were special friends in the small share group from church. They moved back to Indiana in the 1980's, but continued to stay in touch.

Bill* & Nell Rittenhouse(s)—Bill (PhD) was Nassau Bay Baptist's first pastor (for about eight years), then went with Astronaut Jim Irwin as part of the High Flight Ministries, and then returned to Nassau Bay Baptist in the mid-1980's. Bill was a highly-decorated World War II prisoner of war/hero, and his story was presented on the TV series Crossroads. David stays in touch with Nell and supports Global Outreach, the missions organization she and Bill were a part of in later years. David wrote a poem and read it for Bill's 70th birthday celebration, and nearly everyone cried, Bill and Nell in particular. The poem is presented belows.

A Dear Man of God

A Tribute to Dr. William H. "Bill" Rittenhouse, Jr., on His 70th Birthday
from All of His Loved Ones at Nassau Bay Baptist Church
written by Dave Alexander, an Admirer and Friend, April, 1992

Way down in Macon, Georgia, on April 6, 1922,

A preacher couple named Florence and Will bid the Lord a big "Thank You,"

And on that day the world received a very special deal,
For thus began the remarkable life of our own dear Brother Bill.

His siblings, Jim and Peach, arrived to spice those early days,
And love and fun were always there to brighten their PK ways;
As a Melbourne High School athlete, Bill starred in several sports,
Then excelled in pre-med at Stetson U., his history reports.

But then our nation went to war, and Bill could not deny
The call to serve and, as a volunteer, our bombers he did fly;
His family and sweetheart, Nell, he had to leave behind,
But there amidst those terrible days his life's true purpose he'd find.

His plane was downed and in prison camp, as most of us have heard,
He spoke out for Christ and accepted the call to preach the Holy Word;
The Purple Heart and Distinguished Flying Cross he later would receive,
But his greatest reward was the love from those he led in Christ to believe.

Back home the healing miracle continued to unfold,
And the reunion with his faithful Nell was something to behold;
He started back to college and obtained a math degree,
So a missionary teacher he could become as soon as Romania was free.

On December 20, 1944, he married his lady fair,
And ever since in every way she's been for him right there;
The Lord blessed their marriage in a wonderful way and helped make it complete
As He gave them their Sherrie, JoAnn, and Nancy, a trio so pretty and sweet.

Then along came their sons, Rocky, Pete, and John, all the economy size,
And from these three unions six super grandchildren came as no surprise—
Shaun, Christy, Walton, Kim, Grace, and Bridget, oh, what a source of pride,
Each one as special to their Granddad Bill as a wild plum along the roadside.

Though the Romanian dream is still on hold, maybe it is yet to be,
Perhaps someone who kinda' looks like Bill will finally go, we'll see;
But meanwhile God has blessed five churches where as pastor Bill has led,
And as a full-time evangelist many thousands more with the Gospel he has fed.

For Miami, Atlanta, Marietta, Tupelo, and Nassau Bay twice he has cared,
And with Jim Irwin and High Flight around the world the Gospel he has shared;
Royalty, world leaders, and celebrities know him as hero and friend,
But the least of God's children he gladly would help and their rights
    he'd quickly defend.

Much success, thoughtfulness, and optimism have been a part of his life,
And with a great sense of humor and a powerful faith, he has fought
    against sin and strife;
And with gum, ice cream, and VW convertibles, he has helped keep
    young hearts in tune,
And had he been born maybe ten years later, he may have gone
    to the Moon.

A movie was made about this man, and a museum for his family is named,
And many more awards and honors unto Colonel Bill have been proclaimed,
And yet we really have no doubt that what he would choose to record
Would be the names of the many souls that he has won to the Lord.

So, Brother Bill, we conclude with words from deep within our hearts,
With the hope that our love and gratitude they strongly will impart;
You've blessed our lives, you've been our friend, and for sure you've
    caused us to see.
That as long as we truly trust in God, "The best is yet to be!"

Earl* & Margaret Smith—They were directors of the married young adults department in which David and Sandy taught Sunday School. Earl, a Baylor grad and NASA guy, was the chairman of the deacons when David was vice-chairman. They made the trip to attend Sandy's memorial service.

Harold and Judy West(s)—They are both Baylor grads (as well as their daughter and son, Katie and Barry) and were part of the small share group from the church. Harold was a pilot and Judy an excellent pianist/teacher. In the mid-1970's, she composed a marvelous piano medley entitled, "The Life of Christ," which David suggested and helped her organize, and she played it all around the Houston area for many years. A sonnet David composed for her 40th birthday party is presented below.

A Sonnet for Judy
(On Her Fortieth Birthday)

Our Dearest Friend, your time has come at last
For life to really start, or so they say,
But surely you'll proceed as in the past
To spread God's love in your own special way.

Your years to now have brought much joy and love
Through family, friends, and times of faith and cheer,
And through your music talent from above,
You've blessed us all in ways we hold so dear.

But most of all you've been a Christian friend,
An inspiration, giving God the praise,
And as always you surely may depend
Upon our love and prayers in coming days.

Now may our Lord bless you your whole life through,
And may you know His will in all you do.

From All the Gang
Written by Dave Alexander
November 7, 1980

Gene* & Ruby Wright—Gene, a big kidder, was with NASA in the early years, and they both later sold real estate. Ruby's large tub of banana pudding was always a favorite at the church suppers.

Other Nassau Bay Baptist friends (listed alphabetically by last name) are/were Charles (MD) & Anna Barnes, Tim & Joyce Crawley, Wendell Davis, The David (PhD, pastor) Fannins, Rocky & Sherrie Forshey, John* & Helen Ginga, George & June Hare, Mike & Margaret Harreld, Preston & Esther Haynes, Gene* & Hazel Holiday, Tommy (top NASA manager) & Shirley Holloway, Bob* & Mary Bob* Ingram, Tom* & Katy* McElmurry, Jerry* & Carole O'Neal, Bob (house builder across Texas) & Doylene Perry, Larry & Sharon

Reel, James and Leah Rhames, Bob* & Ann Rubion, Jerry & Linda Willman, and Sky & Kitty Woods.

4.8.4 Other NASA-Area Neighbors and Friends

Johnny* & Daisy* Arolfo(s)—Neighbors behind; gave a lot of fun parties.

Sam & Mary Alice Beaty—Sam played bass guitar for The Master's Vessels at various times.

Bill* & Frances Brown(s)—Frances was special school teacher friend of Sandy and remained friends through the years.

Ray* & Rusty Butler—Helped with Prop 13 actions to slow rise in League City taxes.

Lenny and Sue Cruse—Subdivision neighbors; he did David's first will free of charge, and she was school choir director and daughter of movie cowboy, Bill Boyd.

June Ford—Lived in same apartment complex with David and Sandy in Dickinson in early years, and friendship remained through the years. Milli nicknamed her "June Bug."

Darren Foster(s)—Neighbor kid across the street, and good friend of Greg.

Jim & Greta Hockersmith—Subdivision neighbors who were very thoughtful; Greta also taught with Sandy for a while.

Jim* & Trudy Hozek—Subdivision neighbors who helped with political endeavors.

Charlie* & Diane Hutzler—Houston couple who were friends through the Tom Jankowskis.

Ed & Dolores Kenyon—Subdivision neighbors; he worked at NASA and she was teacher, and their two daughters are Baylor grads.

Bob & Nancy Mason(s)—Next-door good, helpful neighbors.

Jerry & Pat Mayfield—Substitute tenor for The Master's Vessels a few times.

Kyle & Mary Lynn Morell—Subdivision neighbors; he was David's tennis doubles partner for several years for friendly subdivision matches.

Les* & Geneva* Seright(s)—Next-door good, helpful neighbors.

Huey & Barbara Strogner—Subdivision neighbors; she and Sandy were walking partners, and they made the trip to be at Sandy's memorial service.

Woody* & Ann Watson(s)—Next-door good, helpful neighbors; Ann and David enjoyed sharing jokes.

4.8.5 Other Baylor Friends

Bob Bustin—Football linebacker in mid-1950's from Kilgore; generous Baylor supporter.

Clyde & Maxine (PhD) Hart—Baylor head track coach for 40+ years, and also Olympic coach for several Baylor trackmen; in Hall of Fame and Wall of Honor; he and prof Maxine are Four-Ever His fans.

Larry Hickman—Football fullback in mid-1950's from Kilgore; played pro football and in Baylor Hall of Fame; also great vocalist.

Ed Hohn—Special law school friend of Milli, who became friend of David and Sandy; worked his way through college and law school, then became very successful attorney.

Jerry (M.D.) & Mary Marcontell—Football end in mid-1950's; helped show David around Baylor during his recruiting visit; friends through letterwinners' association.

Hugh* & Rinky Sanders—Friends through Dutch & Betty Lou Schroeder; he was head of Baylor coral music department.

Olan & Sherry Webb—Their daughter was a sorority sister of Milli at Baylor, and David and Sandy became friends with them through the daughters. They made the trip from Beaumont to Sandy's memorial service.

Royce & Cyntha West—Royce was outstanding football lineman in early-1960's, and Cyntha (PhD) has been in Mrs. America contests.

4.8.6 Other Special Co-Workers at NASA

Bob Becker—Section Head for orbital mechanics and rendezvous work during Apollo

Jerry Bell—Worked with David in development of nominal and contingency rendezvous plans for Apollo

Aldo Bordano—Ascent design manager; threw great parties at his home

Ernie Fridge—Math/physics guy who was tennis buddy of David

Leroy Hall—High-level manager and also Baylor grad

Marty Jenness—Consumables section head and fun guy

Sandy Johnson—Barrios CEO who was friend and short-time boss of David (also see section 1.3.18)

Gene Kranz—Apollo 13 flight director and later Director of Mission Operations

Chris Kraft—Director of Flight Operations during Apollo and later Center Director

Ed Lineberry*—Branch Chief for rendezvous analysis during Apollo; The Master's Vessels sang at his memorial service.

John Mayer*—Division Chief of Mission Planning and Analysis during Apollo; David spoke at his memorial service.

Cathy Osgood—One of few female NASA engineers in the early days, and a good one

Bob Regelberge—Co-worker who was best amateur golfer in area; he and wife threw great parties.

Jerry Shinkle—David's NASA section head when David worked for Barrios; he and wife were also church friends at Nassau Bay Baptist.

Bill Tindall*—Director of Data Systems and Analysis Directorate in late-1970's when David was on his staff; also see Section 1.3.3

4.8.7 Other Friends

Jon Harvey—Original tenor for Thee Mobb Quad (that became Four-Ever His) but moved to Arkansas in 1999.

The Don Hicks—The family that owns and operates the Mayan Dude Ranch in Bandera, Texas, where the Alexanders have vacationed more than a dozen times.

Pearlie Lewis—Secretary of the organization in which David worked at the Naval Ordnance Lab in Corona, California; she and her family were very sweet and helpful to David.

5

Final Remarks

The following are David's final remarks for this book concerning his overall life. "I have had a wonderful, greatly-blessed life. In spite of some very difficult times, and although I am now bent by arthritis and slowed by heart disease, I would not trade my life for a life with 100 years of great health guaranteed but without the love and blessings I have experienced. In my opinion, I have received far more than my share of love and blessings and honors, thanks in large degrees to my wonderful wives, children, grandchildren, parents, relatives, and friends, and to God's love, mercy, and grace. After being told in my early-30's that I would be fortunate to live to age 50, I have counted each new day a blessing. When I do finally head for higher ground, I hope it can be said of me that I was a good Christian, husband, father, grandfather, son, son-in-law, brother, relative, friend, citizen, and worker; and that my overall life earned for me the title of Christian gentleman-scholar-athlete. To God be the praise and glory!"

6

Photos (including information about David's size and other physical characteristics)

David grew up quickly in stature. He was 6' tall by the 6th grade, about 6" taller than most of the other guys his age. By his freshman year (age 14), he was at his full height of 6'3" and weighed about 165. During his junior and senior years in high school, he weighed about 185 during football and basketball and 175 during track and baseball. He pretty well remained in this weight range during college. His maximum weight during adulthood has been about 205, but he has averaged about 190 during the last few years. However, the curvature caused by arthritis has pulled him down to about 6'.

David has medium-blue eyes and had dark brown hair until it started turning gray in his late-40's. By age 55 he was totally gray, but still has a full head of hair.

Baby David   **Junior High School**   **High School Senior**

Senior at Baylor   **NASA Engineer**   **Retired (Age 62)**

First Wife, Sandy, at about Age 50

David & Sandy in Their Early-40's

Second Wife, Virginia in Early-60's

David & Virginia on Cruise in 2003

Little Milli

Milli in Her 20's

Milli and Laura

David I and David II

Little Greg

Greg in His 20's

Greg, Cathy, Caitlin, & Megan

Virginia's Children, Julie & Ron

David's Parents, George & Olga, 1935

White Oak High School's
State Championship Track Team
Spring of 1958

White Oak High School's
State Championship Football Team
Fall of 1957

White Oak High School's
State Championship Basketball Team
Spring of 1957

Baylor-Bound High School All Stars

Baylor Freshmen Speedsters 1959

David in 1958 with Legendary Texas High School Coach, Gordon Woods (David's Texas High School Coaches' Association All Star Coach)

David in 2005 with 200 and 400 Olympic Champion, Michael Johnson

Baylor University's
**Southwest Conference Championship
Track Team**
Spring of 1960

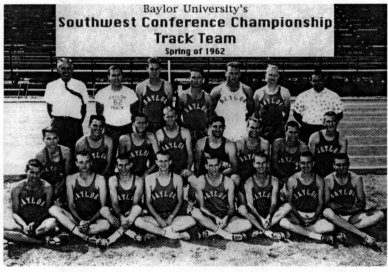

Baylor University's
**Southwest Conference Championship
Track Team**
Spring of 1962

Baylor Trackman, David

Old Baylor Bears, David, Tommy, and Sid

Wall of Honor Speech

Greg, Virginia, David, & Milli on Wall of Honor Night

David receiving NASA Award from NASA Legends Gene Kranz & Aaron Cohen

David with Buzz Aldrin in Tyler in 1999

Original The Master's Vessels Quartet in Early-1980's

The Master's Vessels Quartet (with Wives) in Early-1990's

Thee Mobb Quad Quartet in Late-1990's

The Four-Ever His Quartet (formerly Thee Mobb Quad), 2005 Photo

7

Other Poems, Writings, Etc.

David has composed 60 or more poems, songs, and other writings during his adult years. Some of these (for which copies could be found) that were not included within the earlier sections are presented in this section (along with one poem that was written for David's 40th birthday by a friend, Don Carnes).

7.1 WORDS FOR DAVID'S 14 ORIGINAL SONGS (IN THE ORDER THEY WERE WRITTEN; THE DEDICATIONS OF THE INDIVIDUAL SONGS ARE INCLUDED IN SECTION 1.5)

I Am on My Way to the Glorious Day (1953)

Verse 1:
In this life below (in this life below)
We just cannot know (we just cannot know)
Why there's sorrow and pain (why there's sorrow and pain)
And the wicked seem to gain (yes, they seem to gain),
But 'twill soon be o'er (it will soon be o'er)
When we reach that shore (reach that golden shore),
Where all sorrow will end (all sorrow will end)
And new life will begin (new life will begin);

Chorus:
I am on my way (I am on my way)
To the glorious day (the promised, glorious day)
Where the golden bells ring (those golden bells ring)

And the angels sing (yes, the angels sing),
I will worship the King (I will worship the King)
And forever I'll sing (forever I'll sing),
I am on my way (yes, I'm on my way)
To the glorious day (the promised, glorious day).

Verse 2:
There with loved ones and friends (redeemed loved ones and friends)
There'll be praise without end (joyous praise without end),
With the saints of old (all the saints of old)
On the streets of gold (the marvelous streets of gold),
And the mansion I'll see (the beautiful mansion I'll see)
That He's built for me (that He's prepared for me),
When I see His face (when I see my Savior's face)
I will have finished the race (I will have finished the race);

(Repeat Chorus with Tag and Ending)

Tag:
I will worship the King (I will worship the King)
And forever I'll sing (forever I'll sing),
I am on my way (yes, I'm on my way)
To the glorious day (the promised, glorious day).

Ending:
I am on my way (yes, I'm on my way)
To the glorious day (the promised, glorious day).

Sometimes I'd Like to Go Back (October 1984)

Verse 1:
When the troubles and trials of today tend to drive all the joys of life away,
And we fear for the future of our land, with corruption and sin on every hand;
We may wish for another time and place when the world knew a calm and
    slower pace,
When the children could pray in school each day, and the Bible was used to
    show the way;

Chorus:
Sometimes I'd like to go back (yes, I'd like to go back),
To the days of our fathers and mothers so dear,
When honor and truth and courage and faith were the strength of our land,
But the Lord put me here (yes, He put me right here),
And He promised great blessings, joy, and peace,
If I'd give Him my all (if I'd give Him my all)
And place my life in His hands (place my life in His hands).

Verse 2:
Take me back to baseball and apple pie when the National Anthem
    made folks cry,
And songs about trains brought many a thrill, and a handshake was used to
    bind most deals,
When a marriage and family brought great pride, and the Christians stood
    boldly side by side;
Yet, today it is truly well with my soul for I know that my Lord's still in control;

(Repeat Chorus, then do Ending: So I'll give Him my all and place my life
    in His hands.)

Thank You, Jesus, for Calvary (April 1985)

Verse 1:
I was once so lost in sin, I had no peace and joy within,
Faith and hope I did not know, yet my Jesus loved me so,
Then one day I saw Him there on the Cross my sins to bear,
That blessed day He washed my sins away;

Chorus:
Thank You, Jesus, for Calvary, where You suffered and died for me,
Greater love there could never be, I will praise You through eternity.

Verse 2:
When they nailed Him to the tree—oh, what pain, what agony,
For all mankind He bore the shame—yes, we all deserve the blame,
But as the blood flowed from His side, "Father, forgive them," my Savior cried,
And some sweet day there face to face, I'll say;

(Repeat Chorus, then do Ending: Thank You, Jesus, for Calvary.)

My Crown at His Feet (April 1986)

Verse 1:
In the Bible we're told of the Heavenly crowns
We may earn as we serve here below,
Then one day we'll receive them in that City of Gold,
Oh, what joy and contentment we'll know;

Chorus:
I'm gonna walk down those golden streets,
My mom and dad and all the saints there I'll greet,
But first of all I'm gonna thank my dear Savior and King,
And kneel before Him and place my crown at His feet.

Verse 2:
Soon our sorrow and pain here on Earth will be o'er,
No more trouble, confusion, and hate,
I will sing, "Hallelujah" and shout "Praise the Lord!"
As I walk through the great Pearly Gates;

(Repeat Chorus twice, then do Ending: Yes, Praise God, I'll place my crown
at His feet.)

Let My Life Reflect Your Love (January 1987)

Verse 1:
In this world of pain and trials I so often go astray,
But my Lord is always there waiting in love to show me the way;

Chorus:
Lord, please wash my sins away, help me start anew today,
Fill me with Your Spirit and power from above, let my life reflect Your love.

Verse 2:
If you do not know my Savior, if you long for joy and peace,
Simply give your life to Jesus, He'll give you love that never shall cease;

(Repeat Chorus, then do last line of Chorus as Ending)

It's Time We Pulled Together (June 1987)

Verse 1:
The world is watching each day through to see exactly what we do,
So we must point them to our Father up above,
And as we praise and serve the Lord, we should strive for one accord,
For they will know that we are Christians by our love;

Chorus:
It's time we pulled together, it doesn't matter whether
We would lift our hands or fall on bended knee,
As long as Christ is King, His praises we must sing,
And someday all together in Heaven we will be.

Verse 2:
It's time for us to realize that we should never criticize
When fellow Christians worship in a different way,
And should a fellow Christian stumble, with the world we should not grumble,
But for him each day we earnestly should pray;

(Repeat Chorus)

Verse 3:
There're many churches all around who claim that they are Heaven-bound,
And some may argue that they'll be there all alone,
But Jesus surely died for all who will heed salvation's call,
His precious blood was shed for all sinners to atone;

(Repeat Chorus twice, then do Ending: And someday all together in
    Heaven we will be.)

I'm Excited (July 1987)

Well, I'm excited, for Jesus saved my soul,
And I'm excited, He cleansed and made me whole,
Well, I'm excited, He gladly shows me the way,
And I'm excited, He gives me joy each day,
Well, I'm excited, He gives me all that I need,
Well, I'm excited, He adds great blessings indeed,

Well, I'm excited 'cause He's given me great Christian friends,
Well, I'm excited 'cause I know someday all sorrow will end;

Chorus:
Well, I'm excited and I just can't seem to keep it inside,
The love of Jesus I just really can't hide,
I want the world to know that He set me free,
And that He's coming back so there in Heaven with Him I'll ever be;
Oh, my friend, if you don't really know what I say,
If you will trust Him, He will save you today,
Then you will know the joy and peace that only Jesus can give,
And with His love and great excitement you forever shall live.

Verse 2:
Well, I'm excited, His Holy Spirit's in me,
Well, I'm excited, like Him someday I shall be,
Well, I'm excited, for He has gone to prepare,
Well, I'm excited, I'll have a mansion up there,
Well, I'm excited 'cause I'm a child of the King,
Well, I'm excited, His wondrous works I must sing,
Well, I'm excited and I want the world to know what He's done,
Well, I'm excited 'cause the victory in Jesus is won;

(Repeat Chorus, then do Ending: Yes, with His love and great excitement
     we forever shall live, live, live, live, live—we forever shall live!)

Precious Lord, in My Heart I Love You (August 1987)

Chorus:
Lord, I thank you and Praise You for all that You do
For I know that all blessings come from You,
And though sometimes my life is not faithful and true,
Precious Lord, in my heart I love You.

Verse 1:
As I wake to start each day, I know my Lord will show the way,
If only I will seek His will, His constant presence I will feel,
And through His power and His grace, the world's temptations I can face,
Oh what joy, what peace, what love, it's so real;

(Repeat Chorus)

Verse 2:
What a price He paid for me when He died on Calvary,
He gave salvation full and free so I with Him could ever be,
He is my master and my friend, my praise for Him shall never end,
Hallelujah, in Christ I have victory;

(Repeat Chorus, then do Ending: Precious Lord, in my heart I love you.)

Through Faith By Grace (May 1988)

Verse 1:
Mankind often misses the true meaning of the Cross,
He decides that his good works can pay Salvation's cost,
But the Gospel's true Salvation is a gift that we receive
When we give our lives to Jesus, and through faith we believe;

Chorus:
Through faith by His marvelous grace we are saved,
We're redeemed by the shed blood of God's only Son,
We will praise Him and serve Him for His mercy and His love,
For the victory in Jesus is won.

Verse 2:
Yes, the price for our pardon was paid for you and me
When the blameless Lamb of God died on Calvary,
But He arose, and He's alive, and joy and peace He'll give each day,
When through prayer we live by faith, He will gladly show the way;

(Repeat Chorus, then do Ending: Yes, we'll praise Him and serve Him for
    His mercy and His love, for the victory in Jesus is already won.)

He's in Control (November 1990)

Verse 1:
In this journey here below there's so much we do not know,
And sometimes our pathway seems so sad and hard,
But the Bible makes it clear that we should never doubt and fear,

For all things work for good for them that love the Lord;

Chorus:
He's in control (He's in control), He's in control (He's in control),
Lift your voice and praise the Lord, He's in control,
When the future's looking dim, put your faith and trust in Him,
Look above, receive His love, He's in control.

Verse 2:
In the Word we're often told of how He blessed the saints of old,
And of the wondrous miracles He did bestow,
And let us surely not forget our own wants and needs He's met,
And when His Holy Spirit fills us we will know;

(Repeat Chorus twice, then do Ending: Look above, receive His love,
    He's in control.)

When He Gave His All for Me (March 1991)

Verse 1:
In a stable in Bethlehem God's only Son came down to man,
The prophecies He all fulfilled, yet very few would understand,
His sinless life, the miracles, He spoke the truth, He showed the way,
Then He became the Lamb of God and gave His all for sin to pay;

Chorus:
It was there on the old rugged Cross at Calvary
Where my Jesus took my sin, and He died to set me free,
Now I have given to Him my life and in His Kingdom I'll ever be,
For He bought me with His love when He gave His all for me.

Verse 2:
He chose to do His Father's will, He was betrayed, He was denied,
Though they could find no fault in Him, "Crucify!" they loudly cried,
He could have called the angels down, but victory that day He sealed,
Oh, He was bruised for our iniquity, and by His stripes we are healed;

(Repeat Chorus, then do Ending: Yes, He bought me with His
    love when He gave His all for you and for me.)

Eternal Day (June 1994)

Verse:
This Master's Vessel sails upon life's sea,
Jesus is my captain, He is guiding me,
I have set my course for the Golden Shore,
Where the Light of Love shines forevermore;

Chorus:
I am on my way, Yea-a-a, with a Heavenly song, Oo-oo-oo,
I am on my way, Yea-a-a, and it won't be long,
Though sometimes the storms (of this life) blow this ship astray,
I will soon be home (I will soon be home) to eternal day.

(Repeat Chorus, then do last two lines of Chorus as Ending.)

Men of Old (September 1996)

(Based on a poem written by Betty Gilley)

Verse 1:
Now, Abraham is like the father of all of us here today,
And Moses climbed the mountain to hear what God would say,
King David wrote great songs of praise—they're still the best around,
And Joshua fit the Battle of Jericho, and the walls came a-tumb-lin' down;

Chorus:
We know about those men of old, we read what they did say,
That Jesus Christ would come to Earth and for our sin He'd pay,
We love those Bible characters, they helped to lead the way,
And all together with them we'll be on that glorious day.

Verse 2:
Yes, Jesus had twelve apostles to help Him way back then,
To heal and feed the multitudes and turn their lives from sin,
Ole' Peter whacked off the ear of that guy who tried to take Jesus in,
Saint John, on Patmos, before he died, said Jesus would come again;

(Repeat Chorus, then do Ending: Yes we'll all be together when Christ returns there on that glorious day, day, day, day, on that glorious day—oh, yeal!)

Without Faith We Cannot Please Our Father Up Above (August 2001)

Verse 1:
We have heard of the great faith of the saints so long ago,
How they trusted and obeyed though their future they did not know,
And today we must have faith when with trials we are beset,
We must claim what God has promised, and this truth must not forget;

Chorus:
Without faith we cannot please our Father up above,
Without faith we cannot know the wonder of His love,
If we knew all the answers and could see all God's ways,
We'd have no faith to please Him, so rejoice and give Him praise.

Verse 2:
There's so much in this life we just cannot understand,
So much sorrow and hatred and sin on every hand,
Loved ones suffer and die long before we think they should,
But we must have faith that all things work for the good;

(Repeat Chorus, then do last two lines of chorus as Ending.)

7.2 SANDY'S MEMORIAL SERVICE PROGRAM

"Let My Life Reflect Your Love".... . The Master's Vessels' recording of a song written for Sandy by David in 1987 during Sandy's initial bout with cancer
Presentation of Roses.... ... Sandy's White Oak classmates
Greeting.... . Rev. Dale Perkins, Minister of Music, Mobberly Baptist Church, and family friend
"Thank You for Giving to the Lord" ... Jeannie Richie, PraiSinger friend
"Oh, How I Love Jesus" #529 (one of Sandy's favorite hymns) ... Everyone singing
"How Great Thou Art" ... Derrith Bondurant, PraiSinger friend
A Tribute to Sandy.... Bob Culpepper, longtime NASA friend

"We Shall Behold Him".... Cindy Freeman, PraiSinger friend
Reflections on Sandy's Life:
>   Dutch Schroeder ... longtime Baylor friend
>   Ken Young ... longtime NASA friend
>   Kathy Lanan ... longtime teacher friend of Sandy
>   Greg Alexander ... son of Sandy and Dave

"The Anchor Holds".... PraiSingers and Praise Orchestra, friend Harold Horn,
>   soloist

Comments and Reading of Poem written by Sandy.... . Rev. Dale Perkins
"I've Just Seen Jesus" .... Jena Wayt and Chip Rye, PraiSinger friends
Promises and Thoughts from God's Word.... . Dr. Laney Johnson, Pastor,
>   Mobberly Baptist Church, and family friend

"It Took a Lamb".... PraiSingers and Praise Orchestra, friend Deborah Gilbert,
>   soloist

"Amazing Grace" ... Thee Mobb Quad: Mark Johnson (comments),
>   Rick Anderson, David Sledge, Clay Perkins (subbing for Dave);
>   Sandy is playing piano on the accompaniment sound track;
>   Sign language by Sue Mitchell, longtime Master's Vessels friend;
>   On last stanza everyone stand and sing: "When we've been there ..." #202

Closing Prayer.... . Dr. Gregg Zackary, Associate Pastor, Mobberly Baptist
>   Church, and family friend

Below are the last few verses of a poem entitled, "To Sandy, My Love," writ-ten by David in June of 1962 about nine months prior to their marriage. The Lord truly granted in a marvelous way the desires expressed within David's poetic prayer.

>   And give us that moment when standing so proud,
>   We'll take vows of marriage before You and the crowd,
>
>   Then grant us the good things that life has in store
>   And help us mold young lives that You can adore,
>
>   And through all the joys and sorrows life brings,
>   Cause us to praise You for all the good things,
>
>   And when we come finally to life's last few miles,
>   Keep our love strong then and give our hearts smiles.

Yes, life is worth living since God up above
Sent me my Sandy and taught me to love!

Sandy truly possessed and constantly manifested
the Gift of Love.

The following are friends who came long distances (several hours) to attend Sandy's memorial service. Others may have attended but failed to sign the register: Jerry Alexanders, Sid Alexanders, David Bennetts, Janice Blavier, Hal Boones, Dottie Cottingham, Bob Culpeppers, Bob Doans, Mary Nell Dornan, Bill Durhams, Gene Easleys, Georgette Ellis, Glynn Fields', Jerry Fergusons, Paul Gilmores, Mike Hackneys, Larry Harbours, Tommy Jankowskis, Howard Jones', Jerry Lanans, Paul LeBlancs, Troy LeBlancs, Ken Meadows', Bill McClearys, Cotton Miles', Earl Millers, Wayne Mitchells, Charles Moore, Moon Mullins', Peggy O'Briens, Bill Porters, Ron Sanfords, Dutch Schroeders, Roy Smalleys, Earl Smiths, Huey Stogners, Ed Wandlings, Neal Watkins', Olan Webbs, and Ken Youngs.

7.3 THANK YOU LETTER TO MOBBERLY BAPTIST PRAISINGERS FOLLOWING SANDY'S MEMORIAL SERVICE

Dear PraiSingers and Praise Orchestra,

I hope you realize how very much you honored our Lord, Sandy's memory, and our family through your presentations and support during Sandy's memorial service.

Many of our friends, most of whom are regularly exposed to top-quality Christian music, told us that they had never before heard such beautiful and inspirational music. Although I knew what to expect, I was greatly blessed by both the quality and spirit involved.

I must tell you about a dream (or vision) I had late that night. As I was unsuccessfully trying to fall asleep, I again began reviewing the memorial service. I suddenly was surrounded by great brightness and beauty. Then I saw Sandy sitting in the midst of other loved ones who had gone on before. She was more beautiful and her smile was brighter than ever. Right beside her was a beautiful young woman who waved at me and said, "I love you, Granddaddy." It had to be Ali.

They were all watching and listening to the memorial service. Sandy was wearing a big, beautiful hat with many multi-colored flowers and ribbons. After each presentation in the service, an additional flower or ribbon appeared in her hat.

When the service ended, she arose and began walking toward an even brighter area. There was so much light that I could hardly watch. As she knelt down before this tremendously bright figure, I realized that her hat had become a crown. She took it from her head and placed it at the feet of the one before her. I could not look into the face of the one there, but I could see nail scars on His feet and in His hands as He placed them on Sandy's bowed head—and I knew who He was.

I can't describe the peace and joy I felt when I opened my eyes. I knew that my wonderful sweetheart was happy and totally at peace in the presence of Jesus.

Thank you for taking the time on a Saturday afternoon to help brighten the crown of My Sandy before she presented it to our Lord. I shall always be grateful.

In His love,
David

7.4 LETTER TO THE WHITE OAK EDUCATION FOUNDATION ACCOMPANYING DAVID'S INITIAL CONTRIBUTION

April 2, 2002

Dear Administrators of the White Oak Education Foundation,

I am privileged to make a donation of $25,000 and become a Founding Platinum Benefactor. Enclosed are my personal check for $20,000 and a check for $5,000 from Sandy's trust fund.

I would like for this donation to be registered as a single donation from "David and Sandy Bingham Alexander."

If appropriate, I would also like for part of the income to go toward scholarships for students pursuing math, science, or teaching curriculum.

Sandy, my late, beloved wife and a graduate of the White Oak Class of 1959, was a school teacher for 27 years in the Houston Clear Lake area. She was one of the most respected and requested 3rd and 4th grade teachers in the Clear Creek ISD. She taught children of the NASA astronauts, scientists, engineers, and top administrators. However, her true calling was to teach and develop "red circle" children, those with emotional/disciplinary problems, and she was especially gifted in this area.

I am a graduate of the White Oak Class of 1958. Although I may be remembered more for my athletic achievements as a Roughneck, I also tried to be the best student I could be. I received a solid academic and leadership foundation at White Oak, a foundation that gave me a great start toward my college degree and toward my NASA career, during which I was vitally involved in putting men on the moon and in designing the Space Shuttle and the Space Station and their operations.

I consider this as an opportunity to partly repay White Oak Schools and teachers for the tremendously valuable investment that was made in the lives of Sandy and me.

Let me also express my appreciation to all of you who have given of your time and effort to organize and manage this worthy endeavor.

Deeply grateful,
David Alexander

7.5 WE ARE SO BLESSED
(by David Alexander, January 1984)

These words are not meant to fill us with guilt but instead to cause true
    thanksgiving
By simply reminding of some of the blessings we have in our everyday living;

So often we slight or just take for granted the wonderful gifts from above
Or maybe forget or just don't take time to give God our thanks and our love;

We live in a land where freedom rings out more clearly than man's ever known,
And God continues to pour out His blessings though sin and problems
    have grown;

Yet, with all the sin and problems we have, our nation to God must be dear,
Where else can man speak and worship so freely without reprisal or fear?

Where else in this world is there such opportunity, where else such success
    and reward?
Yes, many of the "common" things we have most of the world can't afford;

Millions of people in Communist nations for God's Word are begging with tears,
While most of us here have two or three Bibles that haven't been opened in years;

Half of Earth's people have almost no clothes, and many don't have any shoes,
Yet, our four-year-old suits or dresses or cars often really give us the blues;

Three-fourths of Earth's people are hungry right now, and millions have
    nothing to eat,
While our big concern is losing some weight or remembering to eat less red meat;

Most of Earth's people are wandering in darkness with really no hope
    for tomorrow,
While Christ gives us lives that are full and abundant, and one day He'll
    end all our sorrow;

God's given great children, grandchildren, and parents, and many a
    wonderful friend,
But greatest of all he gave us his Son to die on the Cross for our sin;

He loves us so much that He bore all that pain, Salvation's full price to pay.
And just for our trusting and growing in Him, we can have peace and joy
    each day;

And just for the asking, our spirits He'll fill and truly cause us to know
That we are His own and always will be—oh, He loves and blesses us so.

7.6 CONVICTIONS OF CARNEY CHRISTY (by Dave Alexander, May 1975)

Note: This poem is dedicated to those of us who have struggled or are struggling with certain sensitive areas of our spiritual lives. The poem is meant to be a bit humorous, but also deeply serious. It is written with sincere love and concern and with the hope that it will cause spiritual self-evaluation for each one who reads it.

I go to church regularly and give more than most,
    And use temperance toward all things, including the Holy Ghost;

The sermons I like best are simple and sweet,
And my "thing" is to organize and keep things real neat.

I have a nice Bible with references and such,
Although I'm so busy I don't read it much;
But I think it's a good book sent down from on high,
Even though parts of it probably no longer apply.

I very seldom witness—except by example,
But for someone so busy, I think that is ample;
Most of my "lost" friends kinda know where I stand,
And I'd tell them about Jesus if they should demand.

Well, I need more training before I "go out"—
A "win course" or two more should lessen my doubt;
Yes, I should be ready in a couple of years,
After I've figured it all out and conquered my fears.

Meanwhile we've a church staff whom we pay quite well
To stay all prepared the Gospel to tell;
So let them do their thing and leave me to mine,
And things will stay "normal," and all will be fine.

I'll deal with those folks who have already come,
And if they're the right type, I'll encourage them some;
Believe me, there's plenty of church work to do
Just keeping alive things like the WMU.

As for long invitations and all of that praying,
I wonder just what all our visitors are saying;
I prefer more "maturity" and much less emotion,
In fact, I'm embarrassed by all the commotion.

I wish those charismatics who raise hands and shout
Would either settle down or consider getting out;

As to whether they're faking, I really don't know,
But I'm sure it'll mean trouble—Dr. Criswell told us so!

Of course, I'm not one of Paul's latter-day types
Who quenches the Spirit and continuously gripes,
Who claims to be Christian but denies His great power—
But I do feel that no service should last more than an hour.

Oh, I've thought about giving it a much closer look,
And maybe even delving deeper into the book,
But right now I'm so busy, it must wait for a while,
Besides I couldn't possibly change my lifestyle.

Why does it cause trouble if it's sent from above?
Yet why do those who believe it seem to glow with God's love?
Is there faith and power that I've never known?
And even if so, do I dare to be shown?

Have I asked the Holy Spirit to show me the way
Or have I based my beliefs on what others might say?
Why have I lacked true victory and joy so long?
Are they just not for me—could I possibly be wrong?

7.7 BROTHER DAVE
(by Don Carnes, for Dave's 40th birthday celebration, November 22, 1979)

As the clouds suddenly parted, a voice did decree,
"On this special day Brother Dave is to be;"
The angels rejoiced in great Heavenly bliss,
But the world surely asked, "Are we ready for this?"

His childhood was normal in a small Texas town,
At leaving, his goal was to become quite renown;

Satisfying this goal was like from a child taking candy,
All he had to do was marry sweet Sandy.

Sandy said "Yes" and it's a good thing she did
'Cause her good looks were transmitted to their kids;
A Bear he became and a Bear he'll remain,
On the grid, court, and track he gained great fame.

Dave knew that in sports he had to play,
How else could he the pretty girls sway?
He's not saved his best until the "fortieth" quarter,
He once was an athlete, now just an athletic supporter.

Actions like these made Dave who he is,
A man of great talent with the world being his;
He chose voice in music instead of piano,
And became in his quartet the world's lowest soprano.

This was unusual as you'll quite agree,
But Dave is unusual as surely you see;
He loves to eat in and he loves to eat out,
It's amazing to me that he's not at all stout.

Dave's quite a guy and makes a great friend,
And he'll fight tooth and nail right to the end;
He's lost only one fight in his entire life,
And that's when he slipped running from his wife.

As a NASA employee, he's among the best,
And no one can top him at taking a rest;
His abilities have gained him a management position,
And he's had to become a first-line magician.

"Type that memo, sort that mail,"
Come his directions, piercing as a nail;

"Don't gripe or relent, follow the 'reg',"
He shouts his commands to Milli and Greg.

Dave's one in a million, thank God for that—
The mold for him God did take back;
As a poet, he's no Longfellow, you know,
Yet on everyone's 40th, he's stolen the show.

We've loved this dear friend right from the start,
Charismatic in nature and giving in heart;
There's none to be found throughout this land
That can come even close to being such a great man.

Happy 40th, Our Friend, Dave,
from Don and All the Gang

978-0-595-44555-4
0-595-44555-1

Printed in the United States
96541LV00002B/412-459/A

9 780595 445554